Real Enterprise-Architecture
Beyond IT to the whole enterprise

Tom Graves
Tetradian Consulting

Published by
Tetradian Books
Unit 215, Communications House
9 St Johns Street, Colchester, Essex CO2 7NN
England

http://www.tetradianbooks.com

Initial release (e-book only) by Tetradian Consulting: April 2007
First published: May 2008
ISBN 978-1-906681-00-5 (paperback)
ISBN 978-1-906681-01-2 (e-book)

Contents

Acknowledgements

Amongst others, the following people kindly provided comments and feedback on the early drafts of this book: Daljit Banger (White Knight Consulting, UK), Bill Branson (Whiteboards That Work, US), Shawn Callahan (Anecdote, Aus), Adrian Campbell (Ingenia, UK), Jane Chittenden (Format Design, UK), Roland Ettema (LogicaCMG, NL), Sandra Fields (NSW DoCS, Aus), John Forrest (Holocentric, Aus), Ken Harper (Gartner, UK), James McGovern (ArchitectBook, US), Helen Mills (Australia Post, Aus), Robert Phipps (NSW DoCS, Aus), Liz Poraj-Wilczynska (Brockhampton, UK), Roy Roebuck (One World Information System, US), Gerry Ryan (NSW DoCS, Aus).

Please note that, to preserve commercial and personal confidentiality, the stories and examples in this book have been adapted, combined and in part fictionalised from experiences in a variety of contexts, and do not and are not intended to represent any specific organisation or individual.

Registered trademarks such as Zachman, TOGAF, FEAF, ITIL, Macintosh etc are acknowledged as the intellectual property of the respective owners.

AN OVERVIEW

About this book

As with many writers, this project arose out of frustration that the book I needed for my work didn't exist. There were plenty about the minutiae of the field I work in – called 'enterprise architecture' – and about some of the frameworks that can be used for small subsets of the work – mainly in IT – but nothing that really covered the full scope.

Over the years, that frustration grew and grew. Until finally I succumbed to what Open Source programmers describe as 'the need to scratch an itch'. And sat down to write.

So this book is about the practice of enterprise-architecture, particularly at the level of the whole enterprise. And it's for anyone who works with the enterprise as a whole: chief officers, strategists, programme management office – roles of that kind.

But what *is* enterprise-architecture, anyway?

What is this thing called enterprise-architecture?

Many business-folk have never heard of enterprise-architecture. Which is not surprising, because most of the literature in the field suggests it's about IT, and *only* about IT. There might be a few throwaway references somewhere to some blurry notion of 'business architecture', but that's about it. Hence of no relevance to everyday business, really.

Which is a problem, because *real* enterprise-architecture isn't much about IT at all. Or rather, although IT is significant, it's only one small part. Turns out instead that that blurry 'business architecture' isn't something that can be skipped over in a rush down to the technical minutiae: it's the *core* of enterprise architecture.

Enterprise architecture is about the architecture – the structure – of the *whole* of the enterprise:

> **Enterprise-architecture is the integration of everything the enterprise is and does.**

Even the term 'architecture' is perhaps a little misleading. It's on a much larger scale, the scale of the whole rather than of single subsystems: more akin to city-planning than to the architecture of a single building. In something this large, there are no simple states of 'as-is' versus 'to-be', because its world is *dynamic*, not static. And it has to find some way to manage the messy confusion of what *is*, rather than the ideal that we might like it to be.

> The gym I frequent in this ancient garrison town is housed in a former NAAFI – a military commissary and entertainment centre, in US terms. It's a relic of the Second World War – and looks it, too. Scattered around in the battered old building there's a bar, a ballroom, a large café, a hairdressing school, a tanning salon, and an ever-changing variety of small clubs and business oddities. Stairs and passageways wander off at random, with side-rooms that don't seem to be used at all; wouldn't be surprised if the keys had been lost for decades.
>
> In short, a mess. But *somehow* it does all work as a whole. Sort of.
>
> Much like most large businesses, in fact. Which is why we need enterprise-architecture.

Grandiose plans won't help us much in making sense of all this complexity. What we need is something simple that will allow us to start small, yet keep a consistent structure as we expand the scope upward to the whole of the enterprise and its environment. So what we need is a *system* for enterprise architecture.

A systematic approach

As a discipline, IT-architecture has been around for the past twenty years or so. So there are a fair few frameworks available, all of them good: Zachman, FEAF, TOGAF and ARIS, to name some of the better-known examples. (You'll find links to these in the Resources section at the end of the chapter.).

But what they're good at, unfortunately, is IT-architecture – not *enterprise*-architecture, in this broader sense. Paradoxically, to go wider, we need something simpler.

The framework I'll use here is about as simple as it gets. We start with a '5Ps' variant of the old Group Dynamics project life-cycle, with *Purpose*, then *People, Preparation, Process* and *Performance*:

- **Purpose** is about the *why* of business – beginnings, intentions, strategy, direction.
- **People** is about the *who*, the teams and skill-sets and relationships we need to put the strategy into action.
- **Preparation** is about *what*, and *where*, and *when*, and *how*: it grounds the ideas and arguments into a concrete plan.
- **Process**, or Practice, puts that plan into action.

- **Performance** assesses the results – not just of the Process, but of the integration of the whole – feeding back into the Purpose for a new cycle.

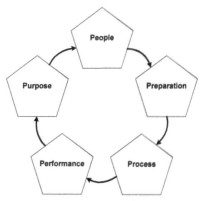

5Ps project-lifecycle framework

Each of these points in the cycle is also a perspective onto the whole, and provides shared requirements that impact on the rest of the enterprise. Mapping these in turn to the issues and artefacts that would be the concern of enterprise-architecture, we find ourselves with a framework that looks like this:

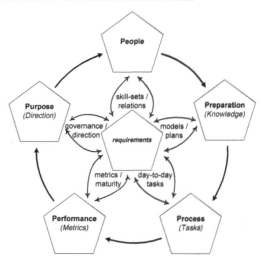

5Ps framework with enterprise-architecture artefacts

If you're familiar with the Open Group Architectural Framework (TOGAF), you might recognise some similarities with the cycle shown in TOGAF's Architectural Design Method (ADM). What's different

> here is that there's no special emphasis given to IT: it's just one part of a much larger whole, almost all of which the ADM bundles into an arbitrary, undifferentiated box labelled 'Business Architecture'. In essence, what this framework does is unpack that box and put everything into its proper perspective.

We apply a systems-principle called *recursion*, and get each view to look at each of the others, and at the integration of the whole. In other words, each view also contains within itself a sense of all the others. This gives us a means to assess *effectiveness* – the overall impact of every part of the enterprise on everything else.

Although they're similar to those '5Ps', we give these sideways views a slight twist, to give us the keywords *Efficient, Reliable, Elegant, Appropriate* and *Integrated*. This gives us a set of views-within-views, which we'll label with two-letter codes as follows:

	Efficient	*Reliable*	*Elegant*	*Appropriate*	*Integrated*
Purpose (*Direction*)	DE	DR	DL	DA	DN
People	PE	PR	PL	PA	PN
Preparation (*Knowledge*)	KE	KR	KL	KA	KN
Process (*Tasks*)	TE	TR	TL	TA	TN
Performance (*Metrics*)	ME	MR	ML	MA	MN

which gives us an overall framework which may look abstract at first, but takes very little effort to translate it into practice. And its consistency and symmetry make it easy to apply across the full scope of the enterprise – which can't be done easily, or at all, with many of the existing frameworks. We'll also see later why and how this kind of iterative, recursive structure supports enterprise agility, usually at a much lower cost than conventional IT-centric forms of enterprise-architecture.

But for now, this provides us with the skeleton for the book: one section for each of the five focus-types, each with five short chapters emphasising specific aspects of effectiveness in relation to enterprise-architecture.

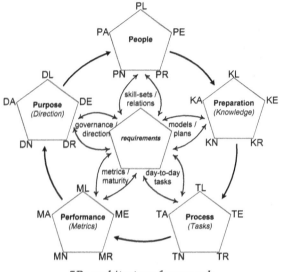

5Ps architecture framework

And each chapter, in turn, has a section on the principles under-lying the issue, followed by suggestions on how to apply those principles in practice, using the same sequence as the main pattern: purpose, people, preparation, process, performance.

Each chapter ends with a brief section on broader usage of the same perspective beyond enterprise-architecture, and includes a list of some suggested additional resources.

'D' group: Purpose - Direction

This is about the far-future focus of business-direction and strategy – typically the preserve of management.

For enterprise-architecture, we need to address the purpose of architecture itself in relation to the enterprise:

- *DA :: The aims of architecture* explores the business drivers – the need to reduce cost and complexity, and to support enterprise integration and agility, that underpin the need for an enterprise-architecture.
- *DN :: Architecture of the enterprise* reviews the development of enterprise-architecture from its roots in IT, and the issues that drive the need to break away from those roots.
- *DR :: The architecture of the everyday* illustrates the need for enterprise-architecture to be relevant to everyday practice, assisting in the day-to-day decisions at the 'coal-face'.

- *DE :: Architecture on purpose* explores the 'audit-trail' of vision, role, missions and goals which provide the anchor for business motivation – and for the enterprise-architecture.
- *DL :: Architecture is a feeling* reminds us that an enterprise is made up of people – so we need to support values, and community, as an explicit part of the enterprise-architecture.

'P' group: People

In the enterprise itself, this is the complicated, almost outside-of-time concerns that people bring to an enterprise.

These are the everyday affairs of HR and the 'people people', but we also need to take them into account in enterprise architecture:

- *PL :: The architecture team* addresses the nature of the enterprise-architecture team itself: skill-sets, mindsets and overall attitudes to the work and to each other.
- *PA :: The politics of purpose* reminds us that everything in an enterprise is underpinned by the complex politics of change.
- *PR :: A problem of power* tackles the subtle balance of power and responsibility upon which the successful implementation of the enterprise-architecture will depend.
- *PN :: The role of the generalist* identifies the difficulties faced by those whose often unnoticed work provides the bridges between organisational 'silos'.
- *PE :: What's the story?* focuses on the narrative knowledge shared by and between people, through which most business meaning is derived.

'K' group: Preparation - Knowledge

This is the near-future emphasis of bringing things and information together to support an upcoming activity – the realm of planners, schedulers, logistics and similar roles.

For enterprise-architecture, it's also about the ideas and images which provide the theoretical foundations for its practice:

- *KE :: Dimensions of architecture* takes a more in-depth look at the business dimensions that underpin the framework.

- *KN :: An emphasis on effectiveness* expands on those 'views' for assessing effectiveness: efficient, reliable, elegant, appropriate, integrated.
- *KA :: Architecture as a way of thinking* introduces the strange realms of system-theory and their immediate practical applications for the agile enterprise.
- *KL :: A question of responsibility* addresses the importance of responsibility-based 'ownership' for the non-tangible assets such as projects, business data and business rules.
- *KR :: The centrality of services* expands the core concept of 'service' in a service-oriented architecture.

'T' group: Process – Tasks

At the point of production, there's a necessary focus on the urgency of the "now!".

The same applies to enterprise-architecture: its practices must support the immediacy of everyday business concerns:

- *TE :: Requirements for agility* surveys some of the Agile methodologies such as XP and DSDM, and how to support these through requirements linked to the enterprise-architecture.
- *TN :: Managing services* describes the role of complementary frameworks such as ITIL, TQM and COBIT, and how to integrate these into a broader enterprise-architecture.
- *TR :: The practice of architecture* goes into more detail on the iterative, recursive process of creating and managing compliance to an enterprise-architecture.
- *TL :: The art of integration* looks at how to use a unifying theme, such as privacy, quality, trust or waste-reduction, in parallel with enterprise-architecture, to increase integration across the enterprise.
- *TA :: What's the SCORE?* introduces a strategic tool to assess potential impacts on overall effectiveness across the enterprise.

'M' group: Performance – Metrics, artefacts and outcomes

In business, this provides the 'rearward view' looking back at completions, deliverables, outcomes of activities – concerns such as sales-fulfilment, after-market monitoring, accounts receivable, statistics and the like.

This is about how the enterprise architecture assists in monitoring enterprise performance – and also the performance of the architecture itself:

- *MR :: Real-time scoreboards* investigates sources for key information in a 'balanced scorecard' to track enterprise performance.
- *ME :: Closing the loop* explores the mechanisms needed for feedback from other areas into the enterprise-architecture, using tools such as After Action Reviews.
- *ML :: People and performance* describes a method to identify 'the ability to do work' across the enterprise, and how to use that information to develop interventions as appropriate.
- *MA :: Measuring maturity* is about the capability of the enterprise-architecture itself, and what needs to be done at each stage to expand its potential.
- *MN :: Monitoring integration* summarises the frameworks and metrics needed to monitor impact of enterprise-architecture on whole-of-organisation integration.

Glossary

The last part of the book provides some additional resources such as a brief glossary of terms.

Using the framework

The aim of this book is that you can apply the framework immediately to your own area of work, and begin to see useful results within a matter of days. Filling in the *detail* of the skeleton will take weeks, months, years, of course: but the skeleton alone is enough to get started on a new view of the enterprise as a whole. Once the skeleton is in place, the detail can be developed by working iteratively, recursively, through the framework in whatever area and to whatever level may be needed at the time. In other words, a "just enough, just in time" approach to enterprise architecture.

Applying the same principle of recursion, this book itself illustrates the framework in action. I've used the same approach as the Agile methodology DSDM – features are limited by time-budget – which in this case has meant allowing myself just two months to get down on paper as much as I can from a couple of decades of work. So I make no pretence that this is some "complete, ultimate guide" to enterprise architecture: it's just one iteration for a much larger, shared body of knowledge – to which someday I hope you will contribute.

But first, read once, quickly, through the whole book; then dip into the framework's toolbox at random, as needed. I'd recommend that you clarify your purpose (Chapters DA to DL) and set up some kind of requirements methodology (chapter TE) before you start; but from then on, almost any order will do. Enjoy!

Resources

- Zachman framework: http://www.zifa.com
- DyA (Dynamic Architecture): http://eng.dya.info/Home/
- TOGAF framework: see http://www.opengroup.org/architecture/togaf8-doc/arch/toc.html
- FEAF framework: http://www.cio.gov
- ARIS methodology: http://www.ids-scheer.com/international/English/products/53961
- ArchiMate enterprise-architecture notation: http://www.telin.nl/index?cfm.project=ArchiMate&language=en

DA :: THE AIMS OF ARCHITECTURE

Principles

What are the aims of the architecture?

This one's straightforward, and usually short and sweet, but it does need to be done *first* – otherwise there's a high risk that time and effort would be wasted. You'll also need to come back and review the results from time to time, for the same reason.

What we establish here are people's expectations of the enterprise architecture. If the aim is to cut costs, for example, or support agility, or reduce complexity, each expectation needs to be documented. This then gives you a list of 'key success criteria' from which to work. *How* you'll achieve such success is something we'll address later, in practice: for now, all we need is that list.

Procedure

Purpose

Identify the overall purpose of the organisation's enterprise architecture.

People

Senior managers, strategists, enterprise-architects.

Preparation

Standard business-analysis tools: whiteboard, meeting-space, pen and paper, time, and access to the required people.

Process

Use standard business-analysis interviews and group facilitation with key stakeholders such as senior managers, to elicit a list of key success criteria.

These are likely to arise first as simple expectations or desires:

- rein in the cost and complexity of IT systems

- support collaboration across the enterprise
- change to a more customer-centric enterprise
- increase adaptability and agility in the marketplace
- improve management of risk and opportunity
- simplify and speed up integration of mergers and acquisitions

For a first iteration, the list above is probably enough: it gives *something* to start with.

In later iterations, you'll need more explicit answers. For each of the 'desires' in the list, ask clarifying questions such as "How will we know when we've achieved this?" and "What would you regard as inadequate / adequate / good / excellent success in relation to this?". Often one desire will be dependent on another: for example, agility is unlikely to happen without reduced complexity. And at the *enterprise* level, success may well depend on interactions across the whole enterprise, making standard silo-based performance measures almost meaningless. What we're after here is 'key performance indicators' and success-criteria that arise from the *whole*, not necessarily from any one part.

These success-criteria become a core part of the enterprise-architecture charter: the measure of its mission, its "capability that will be achieved and maintained indefinitely thereafter".

Performance (artefacts and outcomes)

List of core requirements and key success criteria (KSCs) for enter-prise architecture and whole-of-organisation integration.

Broader applications

This perspective is *Purpose / Appropriate* – a recursive emphasis on the purpose of business-purpose itself. To structure the organis-ation's knowledge about this, see *DE :: Architecture on purpose* (p.21); to explore the emotional base, see *DL :: Architecture is a feeling* (p.30); but here this is more about what the organisation *is* – its identity and reason-to-be.

Does the identity match the purpose? Conversely, does the pur-pose match the identity? Conventional marketing-style analysis and corporate-identity development would be useful here, though if the organisation's power-dynamics will permit it – see *PR :: A problem of power* (p.47) – more value may be gained through large-group techniques such as Open Space or Future Search, or participative depth analysis methodologies such as Causal Layered Analysis, to access and identify the organisation's foundational 'myths'.

Resources

🏯 Large group interventions: see Martin Leith,
www.largegroupinterventions.com/documents/leiths_guide_to_lgis.pdf

🏯 Depth analysis: see Sohail Inayatullah,
www.metafuture.org/Articles/CausalLayeredAnalysis.htm

DN :: ARCHITECTURE OF THE ENTERPRISE

Principles

Having defined the aims of the architecture, we next need to be clear about its scope: just how much of the enterprise will our 'enterprise architecture' address?

This is not as simple as it sounds, because if we're not careful, this innocent-seeming question can lead us into some very murky waters on the shores of organisational politics.

A bit of background is relevant here. Enterprise-architecture first arose a couple of decades ago from an almost desperate attempt to rein in the spiralling cost and complexity of IT-systems – and it's been tainted by that association with IT ever since. Over the years, the scope of the architecture has expanded steadily, from low-level technology, to applications, to data; and from single business units and functions, to across functions, and, now, across the whole enterprise. But for the most part it's still IT – and *only* IT.

> "We're wall-to-wall with architects in here", he said with a grin as he led me to my new office. "Data architects; information architects; infrastructure architects; service architects; Siebel architects; we've got the lot!" From that description, though, seems like anyone who can string two systems together could call themselves an architect...
>
> In reality, describing an IT specialist as a 'messaging architect', or some such, makes about as much sense as describing an electrician as a 'wiring architect'. It's true they do each provide integration across an important subset – a 'view' – of the architectural design, but it's by no means the whole of the architecture. And unless we *do* understand that whole, we'll get nowhere worthwhile.

The problem is that it *isn't* only about IT. From the very beginning, a concern has always been to bring IT into better alignment with business needs – and not allow IT to go its own extremely expensive way, forcing the business to follow rather than to lead. It also doesn't help that IT capabilities have always been over-hyped by each generation of consultants and vendors.

The reality, reflected in almost all enterprise-architecture models to date, is that IT tends toward a kind of 'flatland' view of the world, with low-level technology at the centre, and everything else of decreasing importance the further it is away from that centre. 'Business architecture', if mentioned at all, is little more than a label for 'anything not-IT', and thence all but ignored. In the TOGAF-8 specification, for example, the entirety of that 'everything not-IT' is sketchily dismissed in barely a dozen of the document's 350 pages. But in most cases business is the *reason* for IT's existence: and business doesn't like to be ignored.

So from the business side, there's often a deep resentment at the supposed know-it-all arrogance of IT, and its apparent inability to deliver what business believes it needs; from the IT side, there's often deep frustration that business "just doesn't get it", either in expectations or in awareness of possibilities. It's not a happy mix.

Enter, stage left, enterprise-architecture. It's initially sold to business as a way for IT to bring its own house in order. And although there's a grumble or two about yet another bunch of technical types who appear to do nothing, costs and complexity *do* seem to come down. As long as those 'architects' don't bother us, say business, everything'll be fine.

The catch is that everything in a business-system depends on everything else: we can't just deal with low-level IT in isolation. And as Dana Bredemeyer put it in his influential article, "increasing the scope of Enterprise Architecture to encompass more disciplines increases the benefits to be gained". He listed three maturity-levels of enterprise-architecture:

- *Level 1*: EA = Technical Architecture: reduce IT complexity and costs
- *Level 2*: EA = Enterprise-Wide IT Architecture (EWITA): support collaboration among different parts of the enterprise
- *Level 3*: EA = EWITA + Business Architecture (BA): increase enterprise agility and alignment with business strategy

During these first three phases, even though the architecture team will need more and more links with business, their work will essentially be centred round IT. The team will usually be regarded as belonging to IT only, and would report to the CTO, the CIO, or perhaps the CKO (Chief Knowledge Officer) if there is one.

So far so good – and so IT, mostly. But there comes a time when business needs a new level of enterprise-architecture maturity:

- *Level 4*: EA = integration across entire enterprise: increase adaptability, resilience, management of opportunity / risk; increase synergies between processes and partners

To create this, enterprise-architecture will need to make a quantum jump, to move its scope beyond IT into a much stronger integration with business, and with everything that business is and does. And that's when the sparks will start to fly.

If there's a perception that enterprise-architecture 'is' IT, business resentment is likely to boil over at IT's apparent grab for territory. And IT will understandably complain about what it will see as an unwarranted increase in its workload.

But this expansion of scope *must* happen in order to provide the benefits that business wants. Often the only way that works is for enterprise architecture to become an adjunct of the Programme Management Office, or even report direct to the CEO – in which case, IT may well be unwilling to relinquish control, or resent intrusion by 'outsiders' on what it sees as *its* turf.

Either way, expect a bumpy ride at that point.

Procedure

Purpose

Identify the scope for the enterprise-architecture.

People

Senior managers, strategists, enterprise-architects.

Preparation

Standard business-analysis tools: whiteboard, meeting-space, pen and paper, time, and access to the required people.

Assess the maturity-level of the present architecture before you start – see *MA :: Measuring maturity* (p.123).

Process

The present maturity-level will illustrate the next available steps in the guidelines for developing the enterprise-architecture.

With those guidelines as a base, use standard business-analysis interviews and group facilitation with key stakeholders such as senior managers, to elicit views, opinions and agreement on the scope and authority of enterprise-architecture for the next stage of development.

Be prepared for disagreement and conflict – sometimes fierce – especially at the key transition from IT-centric architecture to a full business-oriented architecture.

Performance (artefacts and outcomes)

Content for enterprise-architecture governance-charter.

Broader applications

This perspective is *Purpose / Integrated* – an emphasis on purpose providing a focus to align the enterprise with itself, and also identifying the 'togetherness' of the enterprise. Its direct counterpart, which focuses on the practicalities and purpose of measuring that 'togetherness', is *Performance / Appropriate* – see *MA :: Measuring maturity* (p.123).

In this perspective the focus is on how purpose can bring the enterprise together into a unified whole. A 'theme' can help to do this, by providing a connecting-point which people can link to in an emotive way in their everyday work – see *TL :: The art of integration* (p.102) – but here it's more about how the business-purpose itself acts as an overarching, unifying 'theme', to underpin strategy development for the whole organisation.

What's needed is a clear articulation of the business Vision – see *DE :: Architecture on purpose* (p.21) – and guidelines as to how to use that Vision as a guide in the kind of 'bumpy ride' of change described for enterprise-architecture above.

Resources

Dana Bredemeyer on maturity-levels: Bredemeyer et al., "Enterprise Architecture as Business Capabilities Architecture", www.bredemeyer.com, slide 10

DR :: THE ARCHITECTURE OF THE EVERYDAY

Principles

What's the purpose of what you will actually *do*? How will the architecture activities help to drive the day-to-day decisions of the enterprise?

This section isn't about the detail of architecture activities – that'll be addressed in *TR :: The practice of architecture* (p.96) – but about the aims and expectations of the architecture's 'customers'. In a sense we'll be covering some of the same ground as in *DA :: The aims of architecture* (p.10), but from the opposite direction: 'bottom-up', from the perspective of individual work-teams, rather than 'top-down', for the enterprise as a whole.

Expectations and decision-types will vary widely, dependent on the industry, the focus of business within that industry, and the architecture maturity-level – see *MA :: Measuring maturity* (p.123). As maturity improves, for example, the emphasis in architecture's relationship with project-teams usually shifts away from 'policing' compliance, and more into an advisory role, of guidance rather than enforcement. Two key decision-areas which apply in almost all cases, though, are *alignment* of projects to the architecture, and cross-project *integration*.

> At that stage in architecture-development, much of our time was taken up with 'alignment reviews', checking project documents for alignment to the intended architecture. All too often we found ourselves undertaking delicate negotiations with projects to try to find some way to bring them back into line – the worst example being the time when separate projects wanted to build *three* different, incompatible RFID item-tracking infrastructures throughout the entire nationwide logistics network... We did have to struggle sometimes to avoid the unpopular image of the 'governance police'; far better, whenever we could, to emphasise the benefits of shared infrastructure and shared systems,
>
> But we were also on the lookout for cross-project synergies, and there was one oddity that caught my eye. A small, unremarked project, for an early-warning system for another part of the logistics network, it had twice been turned down as having a 'negative' business-case – in other words no apparent return on investment. Taken only on its own

> merits, that was fair enough; but we were able to show that, with only minor tweaking, it could act as the 'glue' between six major projects across three different divisions, greatly increasing *their* mutual returns on investment.. At the next cross-division review meeting, that little project gained the nod for an immediate go-ahead.

What we look for in each case are decisions that impact on overall effectiveness – see *KN :: An emphasis on effectiveness* (p.69). In the earlier maturity-levels, the decisions will usually be about a basic quest for improved efficiency and reliability, such as in the use of the TOGAF Architectural Design Method for IT-architectures, or the FEAF architecture Reference Models. At higher maturity-levels, greater gains for effectiveness come from decisions that focus on purpose – see *DE :: Architecture on purpose* (p.21) – or using tools such as SCORE - see *TA :: What's the SCORE?* (p.106) – to align more strongly with business strategy.

Note, though, that the emphasis must be on the practical and the immediate: what day-to-day decisions need architectural support?

Procedure

Purpose

Identify the purpose of the day-to-day architecture activities, and the interactions and impacts these will have with other activities within and beyond the organisation.

People

Selected managers for 'customer' groups, strategists, enterprise-architects, process-architects, programme management office.

Preparation

Standard business-analysis tools: whiteboard, meeting-space, pen and paper, time, and access to the required people.

Assess the maturity-level of the present architecture before you start – see *MA :: Measuring maturity* (p.123).

Process

Use standard business-analysis interviews and group facilitation with key stakeholders such as managers of 'customer' groups, to elicit a list of decision-types – routine and/or project-based – for which enterprise-architecture involvement would be desirable and/or advisable. Examples include:

- monitoring compliance to architecture (especially at project-lifecycle 'gateways')
- providing recommendations to assist projects to be architecture-compliant
- identifying acceptable alternatives for necessarily non-compliant projects
- identifying amendments to project specifications to enable cross-project synergies
- defining and publishing reference-models, design-guidelines, naming conventions, etcetera, to guide project specifications, system implementation and system use

Document the expectations and decision-types in duty-statements for the architecture team and for others such as the programme management office, and as success-criteria for 'service contracts' – nominal or formally-defined – with each of the customer-groups. Also document any decision-types where an escalation may be required – for example, from architecture to programme management office, or to a high-level project review-body – because these may require amendments to governance procedures that would be outside the scope and authority of the architecture team.

Performance (artefacts and outcomes)

Content for enterprise-architect duty-statements; content for governance procedures and issue-escalation procedures.

Broader applications

This perspective is *Purpose / Reliable* – an emphasis on the tasks and the physicalness of business purpose. Its direct counterpart is *Process / Appropriate*, the effectiveness and relevance of day-to-day tasks – see *TA :: What's the SCORE?* (p.106).

The broader application of this perspective is to question:

- Does the chosen purpose match what the enterprise does?
- Does what the enterprise does align with the purpose?
- In what ways does the enterprise balance rules, principles and purpose in its day-to-day decision-making.
- What results and outcomes would we expect at each level of the enterprise between the tasks and the purpose?

One of the best frameworks I've seen for this is a 'results logic diagram' used by all departments of a state government. At the top was the 'government priority', but in effect a well-described Vision – see 'Vision' in *DE :: Architecture on purpose* (p.21). Below this was a set of 'client results' – the outcomes of 'services for citizens', in FEAF terms. Then the measurable outcomes for the department, the 'department results' by which each of these 'client results' would be obtained; and below this, a tree of cross-linked 'intermediate results' – in effect, Missions, in the vision / role / mission / goal format – needed to create the 'department result'. And finally the 'premise' – the assumptions – on which each of the department's service groups was based, linking up to the desired results. True, if misused, the structure could be twisted to justify almost anything; but used properly, the diagram made it easy to see what each part of the department aimed to do, and why.

Try it – construct a results-logic diagram for your own context:

- overall priority or Vision for the broader community
- client result – outcomes for your end-clients
- enterprise result – measure by which you achieve your own outcomes *and* the client outcomes
- intermediate result – tree of linked outcomes of subsidiary Missions
- premise – the core assumptions defining the Role of a service-group
- service-group – the groups delivering specific Missions

Link purpose to practice, practice to purpose, and validate each: that's the aim here.

Resources

- TOGAF ADM: see www.opengroup.org/architecture/togaf8-doc/arch/toc.html
- FEAF Reference Models: see www.whitehouse.gov/omb/egov/a-2-EAModelsNEW2.html

DE ::ARCHITECTURE ON PURPOSE

Principles

How do we know that what we do is 'on purpose'?

No matter what we do at work, it can't be effective unless it in some way supports the purpose of the enterprise. Which means that to do anything effective, we need first to know what that purpose *is*, and have some idea of how to get there.

> Imagine… You're developing a new process, or a new system, or a new strategy, of suchlike, and someone asks you:
>
> **"Why _are_ we doing this, anyway?"**
>
> How would you answer?
>
> How can you be certain that what you're doing *does* contribute to the organisation's purpose?
>
> For that matter, what *is* your organisation's purpose?

The reality is that we can only know we're 'on purpose' when there's a clear *audit-trail* of purpose. In other words, when each *activity* contributes towards a *goal*, which creates or maintains a *mission*, which supports an intended *role* within an overall *vision* of the organisation's world.

That's the audit-trail for business motivation:

> vision ↔ role ↔ mission ↔ goal ↔ activity

Clearly this does need to be a core concern of enterprise architecture, because in effect it identifies the anchors for everything. And we do get *some* hints of this in the existing architecture-frameworks. We'll find it sort of tucked away in the top right-hand corner of Zachman, for example, and in the business-scenarios and references to 'business drivers' in the TOGAF Architecture Design Model. There's also the Business Rules Group's somewhat-incomplete 'Business Motivation Model'. But that's about it: not much we can actually *use*.

Instead, I've found it more useful to start again from scratch, and identify clear definitions and functions for each point in that audit-trail of ends and means, from vision through role, mission and goal. From there, it's simple enough to link to the more easily-identifiable tasks, activities and objectives.

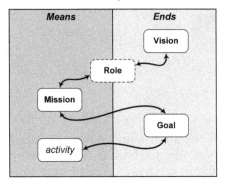

Audit-trail of ends and means: vision, role, mission, goal

There are so many misunderstandings about each of these that it's worthwhile discussing each layer in some detail.

Vision

The Vision is a short, simple statement that describes a desired 'world'. The enterprise commits itself to playing an active role in the creation of this 'world. Some examples:

- "a more sociable world" (Brewers Lion Nathan)
- "boundaryless sharing of information" (The Open Group [IT])

Where most attempts at defining a Vision go wrong is that they look only at the enterprise itself: the classic marketing-style 'vision' of "to be the best this-that-or-the-other".

But to work properly as an anchor for everything the enterprise is and does, the Vision needs to be *much* broader, and much larger than the enterprise itself. It needs to describe a 'world' with space for all the other players we need to make the enterprise succeed – the customers, suppliers, partners, competitors. In effect, *all* the stakeholders will share at least some aspect of the Vision – which is *why* they are stakeholders in that Vision.

It's not something that can be measured, or 'achieved': it just *is*.

The Vision is

- *stable* – it never changes
- *singular* and *universal* – there is only one Vision, applying to everything the enterprise is and does

- *emotive* – it describes 'the passion'; it clarifies desirable and undesirable characteristics for hiring policies; it provides direct motivation – "it's what gets me out of bed in the morning"
- *strategic* – it provides a focus-point to identify 'weak signals' from the complex-domain – see 'Managing complexity' in *KA :: Architecture as a way of thinking* (p.74) – that forewarn of strategic changes in technology, society and the like

The enterprise Vision can't change, because the enterprise would change fundamentally with it – in an all too literal sense, the enterprise would cease to be itself. And the Vision is not abstract, it needs to appeal in a very *personal* way: if we can't connect with it in that literally emotive sense of "getting us out of bed in the morning", we're possibly in the wrong enterprise.

Identifying the Vision: Rule Number One: it's not a marketing exercise! The business-functions are entirely different: a pitch is a short-term appeal to the market, whilst Vision is the unchanging anchor for the organisation itself. *Never* confuse these two functions: mistaking a market-pitch for a Vision can kill the company.

Identifying a valid Vision does take time, because it's not so much a choice as a *feeling* – see *DL :: Architecture is a feeling* (p.30). Look for hints of it in the enterprise's history; in the anecdotes and stories people tell each other – see *PE :: What's the story?* (p.57); and in the real values that people express in their work.

See the examples above for typical phrasing of valid Visions – it's not complicated, but it does need to be emotive in some sense. And to be certain that the phrasing is right, again test the feelings that it elicits. If it works, it should bring out an almost indignant response of "we do it because *that's who we are!*"

Role

A Role describes what the enterprise aims to do *and not do* within the Vision's 'world', as its contribution towards the Vision. It describes where the enterprise fits, as one actor amongst many contributing towards the world of the Vision. Some examples:

- "brewer and distributor" (Lion Nathan)
- "provider of police services for the county of Essex"

Though a Role will often include some kind of boundary, such as processes, overall activities, or geographical constraints, there's no qualifier – no "best of" or "premier provider of" or suchlike. It's just a simple statement about what the enterprise *does* in this Role..

Placing a boundary round what the enterprise does, the Role automatically implies other Roles needed for the Vision-world happen. To take the Lion Nathan example of "a more sociable world", if our Role is "brewer and distributor", we'll need to connect with a variety of other Roles – not just the obvious such as 'customer' and 'supplier' and 'competitor', but others such as 'provider of police services'. Our Vision and Role tell us that these odder intersections with other Roles would be an *expected* part of business – which can 'surface' hidden opportunities, and reduce potential for unpleasant surprises from unexpected stakeholders.

Unlike Vision, the Role does drift and change slowly over time – hence each Role should be subject to regular review. We may find a different set of boundaries to our Role would fit better with our capabilities or Missions; we may choose to change the Role when a new technology makes possible a new Mission; and so on. Yet a Role is neither an 'end', nor a 'means', nor do we ever really 'achieve' it. It's simply what we *do* – what we *choose* to do.

Specifying a Role: A Role expresses a chosen frame or context through which the enterprise means to contribute towards the ends of the Vision. Each organisational unit within an enterprise will play a different Role, or several Roles, but all will contribute towards the *same* Vision. By exclusion, this also clarifies probable Roles of other stakeholders in the Vision-world.

See the examples above for typical phrasing – it's straightforward. Overall, the Role will need to feel more 'considered' than the Vision, more 'thought-through', but it will still be grounded in *feeling*. It should elicit a bright, assertive response of "but that's what we *do*!".

Mission

A Mission describes a capability or service to create, via Goals, and maintain indefinitely thereafter. So it has two distinct phases: the initial phase when it's created; and the subsequent phase of continuous operation. (There's also a third phase for wind-down if and when the Mission ends.) In that sense, it's more like a trade-mission than a one-off military-style mission – in fact the latter is really a type of Goal. For each phase, too, we'll often need different people with different skill-sets, and certainly need different Goals.

In motivation terms, the Mission description's function is straight-forward: it tells us the overall means, the *how*, by which a Role will be delivered, and often also identifies measures to verify successful delivery. Some examples:

- "maintain stocks and deliveries to achieve and maintain 20% market-share for brewed products in ANZ"
- "provide DNA-based forensic evidence facilities for Essex"

Missions must identifiably support a Role and Vision, and *must* be measurable, through the usual collection of key performance indicators, key success criteria, service-level agreements and the like. These metrics tell us whether we're on track in delivering the Role in the Vision-world. But note that a Mission is never actually 'achieved': we measure it instead.

In many cases, Missions are not only about the enterprise itself: they're as much about partners, other Roles in the Vision-world, because those Missions are points of contact with these 'outside' Roles. The metrics associated with the Mission must also monitor and manage that association.

A Mission is also a locus for continuous-improvement processes: its metrics are key inputs to quality-management. And Missions also need regular review, not only against their own metrics, but against the respective Role, because each may change the other.

Specifying a Mission: Both Missions and Goals should be derived via standard project-management or service management methodologies such as PRINCE2, PMBOK or ITIL. Strategy and foresight tools may also be useful: not only standard techniques such as the 'business scenarios' in TOGAF's Architectural Design Method, but also participatory techniques such as Open Space and narrative inquiry, and advanced methods such as Causal Layered Analysis.

A Mission should be phrased to identify the capability or service and its key success-criteria. These *must* be measurable – not fluffy 'market-speak' as "best" or "premier" or suchlike. The phrasing should elicit a response of "that's *how* we do what we do!".

Goal

A Goal is a description of a 'project' with a specific set of deliverables and a target date for completion. (Every transit through a value-chain is a 'project' with a finite goal.) In turn, it identifies a single finite set of activities required in order to support or maintain a Mission. The description consists of two mandatory parts – the deliverables for the Goal, and required start- and completion-dates – and an optional list of additional metrics to be checked on completion. An example:

- "bring DNA database on-line for all Essex forensic units by «*date*»"

A Goal must always contribute toward a Mission – it never exists in isolation. And though we say that the Goal completes at the end of its main activities, there needs to be a brief additional phase to capture 'lessons learned' and other performance information. In Total Quality Management, this is the 'Check' phase. If this phase is skipped, from pressure of other Goals, overall performance may suffer, as it is the only point at which criteria for success or failure may be applied, and the information gleaned in this follow-up phase provides key information for process reviews.

Goals are immediate, explicit, concrete and practical. They also provide clear boundaries of time, space and context, making it easier to concentrate on the task to hand.

Well-constructed Goals provide a useful sense of urgency, of *need* to complete. They're often arranged in hierarchies, with longer-term Goals – such as to create a new Mission – partitioned into smaller Goals through some kind of work breakdown structure. By this means, the same urgency can be maintained through much longer periods – which can greatly increase overall productivity.

Specifying a Goal: See 'Specifying a Mission' above. The key differences are:

- at the end of a cycle, a Goal *completes*, but a Mission *continues*
- measure or review *after* a Goal, but *during* a Mission

A Goal should be phrased to identify the deliverables, the time-boundaries, and optionally the success-criteria. The phrasing should be validated against the classic 'SMART' checklist: specific, measurable, achievable, relevant and time-based.

Common visioning errors

Strategies and tactics implement the paths to the Vision:

- use strategy to review the continuous subtle changes needed in the Role, and create and maintain Missions to match
- tactics define the Goals and activities needed to support each Mission

Successful strategies depend on clear Goals; and Goals depend on clear Missions, Roles and Vision. *A misframed Vision will render strategy unreliable, unstable and error-prone.* Common visioning mistakes include:

- *Role as 'Vision'*: "providers of brewed products to ANZ market" – this confuses ends and means, and invites a "so what?" response
- *Mission as 'Vision'*: "achieve and maintain 20% of market share" – this is self-referential, leaving no room for connection with customers, partners or other stakeholders – invites a "What's in it for *me*?" response
- *Goal as 'Vision'*: "beat Benz!" (Lexus cars) – produces good short-term urgency, but kills motivation stone-dead once the goal is reached
- *desired future-state as 'Vision'*: "our vision for the 'to-be' IT-architecture" – a future-state is effectively Mission-as-Vision

This last is a subtle semantic problem – a different meaning of 'vision', valid in its own way, but not Vision in the sense we're using here. A simple test: if it's temporary, or narrow in scope – such as a 'future-state architecture' – then it's not a Vision.

- *success-criterion as 'Vision'*: "taking a lead in the security of Essex" – this blurs the activities of a Role with the measures of a Mission

The success-criterion in this type is often spurious or unmeasurable – for example, how would you measure "taking a lead"?

- *marketing-slogan as 'Vision'*: "to be the best bakers of the century!" – this form combines every error: role-based, self-referential, goal-driven, spurious measure

It's unfortunate that this erroneous 'marketing-hype' form is the style recommended in many texts and 'standards', including the Business Motivation Model. Be warned: it doesn't work – it simply cannot do the job that a valid Vision needs to do.

With a valid Vision, we should be able to link *every* activity to the Vision, using an audit-trail in the general form:

"This «*activity*» implements part of the deliverables of «*Goal*», to be completed by «*date*», which will assist in creating or maintaining «*Mission*», as measured by «*metric*» and «*success-criterion*», which supports «*Role*», with «*customer*» and «*supplier*», which contributes to «*Vision*»."

A systematic process of visioning provides the means to identify each step of this link.

Procedure

Purpose

Establish foundations for enterprise business-motivation model and framework for motivation 'audit-trail' processes.

People

Enterprise architects, strategists, others as appropriate.

Preparation

Standard business-analysis tools: whiteboard, meeting-space, pen and paper, time, and access to the required people.

Summaries of existing vision, mission, objectives, goals, etcetera and any frameworks linking these to business process and performance.

Research on internet and other sources, for methodologies to create and maintain audit-trails for business-motivation.

Process

In conjunction with strategists and others, review existing materials and methods for creating and maintaining business-motivation audit-trails. If necessary, define or amend motivation reference-models.

Using any appropriate tools, such as TOGAF's business-scenarios, the Business Motivation Model, or the VRMG framework above, identify and document any changes required to improve support of motivation across the enterprise, and monitoring of motivation.

Outline change-requirements to amend metrics and strategy-procedures accordingly.

Performance (artefacts and outcomes)

Vision / role / mission / goal business-motivation framework; content for motivation audit-trail procedures.

Broader applications

This perspective is *Purpose / Efficient* – an emphasis on ensuring that the purpose can make the best use of all of the enterprise's resources. The direct counterpart is *Preparation / Appropriate*, about appropriate knowledge for purpose, though much of it would also apply here – see *KA :: Architecture as a way of thinking* (p.73).

The same principles apply to all aspects of the broader enterprise:

- what is the Vision?
- what are the Roles?
- what are the other Roles that the enterprise – or this part of the enterprise – does *not* do?
- who holds those Roles?
- how do our Roles interface with them? – in other words, through what Missions?
- what are the current Goals for each of those Missions?
- how do these Vision, Roles, Missions and Goals guide day-to-day decision-making?

For the lower-level detail, use a systematic process such as the Business Motivation Model, or a more purpose-built structure of processes such as ITIL (for the IT industry), for example, or SCOR (for the logistics industry). Ensure that, wherever required, a motivation audit-trail can be constructed for *every* activity in the enterprise.

Resources

- Business Motivation Model: http://businessrulesgroup.org/bmm.shtml (adopted by the Object Management Group as a standard – see www.omg.org/technology/documents/bms_spec_catalog.htm)
- Business scenarios in TOGAF ADM: see www.opengroup.org/architecture/togaf8-doc/arch/toc.html
- Narrative inquiry: see Cognitive Edge at www.cognitive-edge.com or Anecdote at www.anecdote.com.au
- Open Space: http://www.openspaceworld.org
- Causal Layered Analysis: see Sohail Inayatullah, http://www.metafuture.org/Articles/CausalLayeredAnalysis.htm

DL :: ARCHITECTURE IS A FEELING

Principles

What values are expressed in the architecture of the enterprise?

In a conventional IT-centric architecture, this kind of question has almost no meaning. In the Zachman framework, for example, the only reference to this is tucked away in the top right-hand corner of the 'Motivation' column. And values in the human sense aren't even mentioned in the TOGAF Architectural Design Method.

But as enterprise-architecture maturity increases, and is required to support more complex concerns such as organisational agility, adaptability and innovation, values necessarily come more to the fore. The reason for this is illustrated well by a slightly different view of the Cynefin model of organisational complexity described in more detail in *KA :: Architecture as a way of thinking* (p.74):

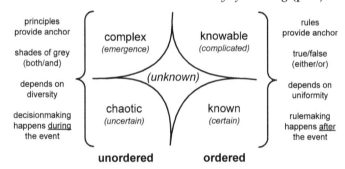

Cynefin model and values

Values and principles might seem a nuisance in the ordered world of the known and knowable domains, but they're the core of business motivation – see *DE :: Architecture on purpose* (p.21) – and are essential for providing guidance in the messy unordered complexity of the real world. Without them, every change and undocumented exception must be covered by some kind of new rule, defined from higher up in the organisation – which *really* slows things down.

What we're doing here, though, is *not* a marketing exercise – it's essential to understand this. What we aim to identify are the *real* values of the organisation-as-community, the principles and values that the enterprise, collectively, does use in its day-to-day decision-making. These can sometimes be a long way from those portrayed by marketing, HR or the public relations department.

> One of our more interesting assignments was a values analysis for a large security organisation. They were aiming to move from a rules-based culture to a principle-based one, to cope with increasing complexity in their operations environment.
>
> The public documents and training materials talked about values such as 'service excellence', 'service innovation' 'professionalism', ' 'a rewarding work-environment', and the like – all fine in themselves, but somehow felt devoid of meaning. And there was no mention at all of the kind of ideals that the members of the organisation *really* lived by, as evidenced in the stories in the internal magazine, and the personal awards listed in the lobby – values such as courage, responsibility, fairness, a willingness to risk self for others.
>
> A bizarre divergence, then, between the supposed values and the real ones – so where did these 'official' values come from, we asked? "Our marketing department made them up", they said. No wonder they were a bit confused about where their organisation was headed...

Once we know what the real values are, we can then adapt the architecture to emphasise some of these values and de-emphasise others, according to the desired direction for the enterprise. This is similar to the design of a user-interface to encourage certain be-haviours and dissuade others, by placing preferred workflows on the opening screen and the exception-workflows deeper down.

But it *must* be done with care, with subtlety, and with respect, because the politics of change are never simple – see *PA :: The politics of purpose* (p.42). In a very real sense, changing someone's values means changing who they *are* – and few people respond well to clumsy attempts at cultural engineering.

> He was one of the best systems specialists in the world – a prime catch for any software corporation. But he certainly wasn't happy about his previous job. "On my first day as a new employee", he said, "they gave me my new corporate t-shirt, my new corporate mug, and my shiny new card of corporate values by which I would live my whole life henceforth."
>
> "What values?", I asked. He gave me a rueful grin.
>
> "Top of the list was 'Maximising shareholder return'." He drained his glass, raised it in wry salute. "Told 'em where to shove their values. I was outta there in a week: went someplace else where they let me be me."

One place where top-down principles and values *can* be safely defined and promoted is in the operation and structure of the architecture itself. For the 5Ps framework we're using here, this section represents the human-factors view on enterprise purpose. In section *KN :: An emphasis on effectiveness* (p.69) this is described as the 'Elegant' aspect of effectiveness – though here it's 'elegant' more in the scientific sense, the simplicity and clarity of a well-balanced equation. These are values that we *need* in an architecture, whether we're aiming to enhance agility or simply to keep down complexity and costs: so embed them explicitly in the architectural frameworks you develop.

Procedure

Purpose

Identify values to be expressed and embedded in the enterprise-architecture, and to be used as a bridge with customers, partners and other stakeholders.

People

Senior managers, strategists, enterprise-architects, selected others from any/all levels throughout the enterprise.

Preparation

Standard business-analysis tools: whiteboard, meeting-space, pen and paper, time, and access to the required people.

Assess the maturity-level of the present architecture before you start – see *MA :: Measuring maturity* (p.123).

Process

Use standard business-analysis interviews and group facilitation with key stakeholders such as managers of 'customer' groups to identify existing principles, values and other collective emotional drivers that can be leveraged to support the roll-out of the enterprise architecture and other change-management, and which in turn would underpin the enterprise-architecture itself.

At higher maturity levels, use narrative inquiry – see *PE :: What's the story?* (p.57) – to elicit actual values promoted and expressed within the work-communities.

Assess the impact of these values on governance for projects, for enterprise-architecture and other aspects of the enterprise.

If changes to existing values are desirable – either to reduce the impact of certain values, or to enhance others which would align more strongly with the intended architecture – develop a cultural intervention brief for use by change-managers and organisational development specialists. (Management of cultural change should not be within the remit of the architecture team.)

Document these drivers and values. If practicable, publish some or all of these findings as an explicit part of the architecture.

Performance (artefacts and outcomes)

Content for enterprise-architecture governance-charter; content for motivation model.

Broader applications

This perspective is *Purpose / Elegant* – an emphasis on the 'people' side of purpose, but also elegance in the sense of simplicity and clarity. Its direct counterpart is *People / Appropriate* – see *PA :: The politics of purpose* (p.42).

The point here is that purpose is *felt*, at a direct, visceral level – something that becomes literally emotive. And it needs to be felt as *personal*, not abstract. This is why commercial organisations that place excessive emphasis on shareholder-value are almost guaranteed to fail: it's abstract, and it's someone *else's* purpose. What *does* work is clarity on values and Vision, as described in *DE :: Architecture on purpose* (p.22): get clear on that, and the shareholder-value will all but look after itself.

Resources

🏛 Role of values in the workplace: see www.valuesatwork.org

📖 Michael Henderson and Dougal Thompson, *Values At Work: the invisible threads between people, performance and profit*, HarperBusiness (2003), ISBN-10 0-86950-471-2.

PL :: THE ARCHITECTURE TEAM

Principles

Who do we need for the architecture team?

The questions and concerns here are straightforward, though the answers will change considerably at differing levels of architecture maturity – see *MA :: Measuring maturity* (p.123). For the earliest stages there may not even be a team as such – more an occasional meeting of disparate specialists – and in later stages the architectural community-of-practice is likely again to be made up of dispersed 'virtual teams'; but in the intermediate stages a tightly-coupled team is essential.

> The make-up of the team is important at every stage, of course, but one of the most pressing concerns is leadership through the transitions *between* each of the maturity-levels. Twice now I've seen architectural development in a very large organisation come to a grinding halt because the then lead of the architecture team could not accept the need for a change in emphasis. In both cases the sticking-point was the transition from level-2 to level-3 – in other words, the shift from an inward-looking focus on technology to an outward-looking emphasis on business alignment for IT-architecture.
>
> In one of the organisations, the lead was quietly promoted sideways to head a different IT team, and was replaced by someone with a stronger business-strategy background – after which the respect and usefulness of the enterprise-architecture grew by leaps and bounds.
>
> But in the other organisation, unfortunately, the lead had gained the personal protection of a powerful patron at board level, with all-too-predictable results. Shielded from change, the architecture team retreated further and further into their known, 'safe' world of technology, even abandoning any interest in data-architecture as they spiralled down into angry irrelevance. Two years later, that organisation had lost almost all of its previous enterprise-architecture capability.

The individual and collective skill-sets will also change with each maturity-level, which we could summarise as follows.

In the initial *technical-architecture stage*, the main focus will be on reining in the cost and complexity of specific IT systems. It's unlikely there would be any distinct enterprise-architecture team;

instead, the architecture – such as it is – would be the responsibility of individual projects, usually with a focus on either the application-layer or the infrastructure layer, though occasionally straddling the boundary between them.

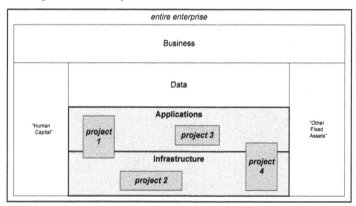

Level 1: enterprise-architecture within projects

There's likely to be little or no focus on the data layer, only a limited awareness of the business layer, and no awareness at all of anything outside of an IT-oriented scope.

The skill-sets needed here are those with a straightforward technical focus: specific applications, specific network configurations, and so on.

Although in some projects there may be a requirement for specialist skills such as enterprise application integration, it's probable that any 'architecture' work will be done only by the project-lead, in coordinating the different technical specialists. There will at least be an awareness that the ability to construct that kind of integration does require a special type of skill.

For the next level, for *enterprise-wide IT-architecture*, a discrete 'enterprise architecture' team is created, usually as the result of issues identified by projects, or from repeated calls by business for some kind of cross-project coordination. In the early stages there may be only a handful of people in the team, but in the later stages there may well be dozens, especially in a larger organisation.

The focus is still strictly IT, but does now extend to include data-architecture. There will be a slightly stronger link with the business layer, particularly if coordination with process-changes is required for configuration of customer-relationship management, or business process reengineering or the like, but beyond that there will still be little if any awareness of a world beyond IT.

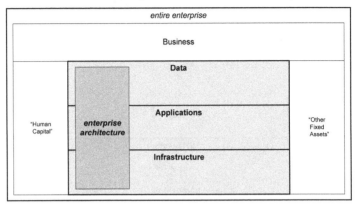

Level 2: bridges data, applications and infrastructure

This period is characterised by construction of reference-models in the FEAF or Zachman mould, so the team will require not only a broad range of technical skills, but the ability to think in abstracts as well as the details of low-level implementation.

A classic danger here, often arising from confusions about the role of frameworks, is for the team to turn inward and wander off into an academic obsession with the purity of models for their own sake. So a key skill required of the team-lead here is the ability to keep a focus on the *usefulness* of the models for cross-project coordination. Without this, the team soon becomes irrelevant to business and even to the rest of IT, and the only useful enterprise-architecture development instead comes from 'transformation'-type projects – an embarrassing situation I've seen in practice in several large organisations.

Integration is usually provided by adherence to a standard frame-work – usually Zachman, at this stage, or an industry-specific framework such as eTOM for telecommunications.

The next stage, *IT-architecture with business-architecture*, is char-acterised by a shift to a stronger focus on the *application* of enter-prise architecture – on methodology rather only on models – and also on a closer alignment with business. The architecture team itself will often shrink radically, as distinct sub-groups for data-, application- and infrastructure architecture are spun off to provide specialist support to projects. There may also be cross-links to new teams dealing with architecture-type issues, such as service-oriented architecture, information-architecture, security-architecture and so on.

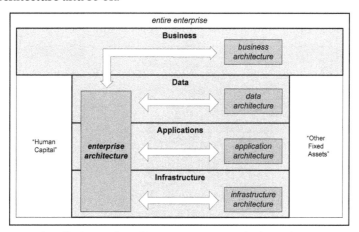

Level 3: distinct sub-architectures, stronger links with business

Freed from project-level architecture, the focus of the remaining enterprise-architecture team shifts to cross-project and cross-enterprise integration – searching for synergies and reducing possible system redundancies. There's stronger awareness of business drivers, and a whole new area loosely labelled as 'business architecture' – even though the term is often misused to mean 'anything not-IT'.

The required skill-sets also change radically: team-members now need to be generalists bridging *across* all the specialist domains, and able to hold the big-picture view in their heads whilst assessing project-level detail – see *KA :: Architecture as a way of thinking* (p.73) and *TR :: The practice of architecture* (p.96). Interpersonal skills also come to the fore, in promoting a more disciplined approach to governance, and in cajoling often-recalcitrant project-leads to comply with the selected architecture principles – though some of this load should be taken over by the programme management office as governance-maturity is further developed across the enterprise.

The whole team is responsible for cross-project integration, guided by a formal methodology such as FEAF or TOGAF.

At the true *enterprise-architecture* level, the role moves 'upward' to become responsible for architecture across the enterprise as a whole – and not merely for the IT subset. (A hint: at this level, if a job-specification includes a reference to any specific technology, such as .NET or SAP or whatever, it's no longer *enterprise* architecture – it's an aspect of domain-level enterprise-*IT*-architecture. It may seem a subtle difference, but it's extremely important here.)

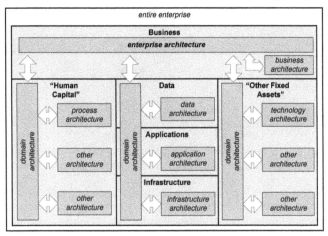

Level 4: coordinates architecture across whole of enterprise

The previous IT-oriented 'enterprise architecture' becomes one of several vertical *domain architectures*, each coordinating the specialist sub-groups working across a cluster of organisational 'silos', partitioned by business function, geographical location or the like.

Where the previous team would report to the CIO or CTO (and probably still does), this new team will usually be attached to a cross-enterprise group such as strategy or the programme management office, or even report direct to the CEO.

For the first time, the focus is truly enterprise-wide. (In the diagrams here I've used the FEAF labels "Human Capital" and "Other Fixed Assets" to indicate these previously-'invisible' aspects of the organisation.) The emphasis is on a much stronger integration with business strategy, and on cross-domain concerns such as increased agility and innovation, reduced time-to-market for new products and services, and improved potential for partnerships to extend the effective boundaries of the enterprise.

Members of this small team need to be strong generalists – see *PN :: The role of the generalist* (p.52) – who are able to listen well, to learn fast, to synthesise ideas quickly in visual or verbal form, and able to build easy relationships with anyone at any level in the organisation and beyond. Although they should usually have a background in a relevant technical or business discipline, they are more likely to call on the team's network of specialist advisers, from within the domain-architecture sub-groups or elsewhere.

Although often associated with the business-strategy group, the roles of the teams are different: strategy defines the desired direction, whilst enterprise-architecture identifies the connections that make the strategy possible in practice.

Procedure

Purpose

Identify the make-up of the enterprise-architecture team, the required collective and individual skill-sets, and recommended collective and individual performance-criteria.

People

Selected senior managers, enterprise architects, lead trainers, HR specialists.

Preparation

Standard business-analysis tools: whiteboard, meeting-space, pen and paper, time, and access to the required people.

CVs and broader interests of existing members and candidates for the architecture team.

Assess the maturity-level of the present architecture before you start – see *MA :: Measuring maturity* (p.123).

Process

Use literature search, and standard business-analysis interviews and group facilitation with key stakeholders such as managers of 'customer' groups, to elicit a list of skill-sets and personal attributes required collectively by members of the architecture team, and by each individual member of the team.

For the earlier maturity-levels, the emphasis will be more on technology- or domain-specific skills:

- *technology/infrastructure architecture*: development of technology principles, standards and patterns that can be shared across multiple systems and solutions

- *applications architecture*: aligning the solutions portfolio with the business and data architectures, and linking applications together
- *data/information architecture*: modelling, classification, integration and management of data, metadata and information, and the business-rules linking them and guiding their transformations
- *business architecture*: modelling and management of processes, workflows, material-flows and the like, and strategy and change-management to guide functional change

Although relevant at all stages, the core *architectural* skills come to the fore at later maturity-levels:

- communicator, change-agent, and creator of social-networks
- modeller and visual thinker
- strategist with foresight disciplines
- fast learner
- principled pragmatist
- consultant and 'troubleshooter'
- 'big picture' thinker

Using the identified maturity-level and individual CVs as a guide, assess the current architecture-team for gap-analysis to identify:

- changes to team make-up: additional members needed, sub-teams split-off, and so on
- additional skills: training required, conference-attendance etcetera
- changes to reporting and line-of-authority: to project-group, to CTO/CIO, to programme management office, to strategy/CEO, etcetera

Develop appropriate strategy and management for any required changes. Where necessary, document these changes in the architecture governance charter.

Performance (artefacts and outcomes)

List of required skill-sets; content for enterprise-architecture job-specifications and performance criteria; gap-analysis and change-management strategy for amendments to enterprise-architecture team; content for enterprise-architecture governance-charter.

Broader applications

This perspective is *People / Elegant* – a recursive emphasis on people *as* people, in all their complexity and difference; on human-factors, such as ergonomics and self-adaptation; and also on simplicity, clarity, the *effortlessness* of elegant design and operation when these all act 'on purpose'.

In this section we've focussed on how these issues come out in the skills and attributes needed for the architecture team. But the same principles and drivers apply to the skills and attributes needed elsewhere:

- what is the purpose? – see *DE :: Architecture on purpose* (p.21)
- what is the scope? – see *DN :: Architecture of the enterprise* (p.13)
- what is the maturity-level? – see *MA :: Measuring maturity* (p.123)

We also need to pay especial attention to the human complexities of politics in the enterprise – see *PA :: The politics of purpose* (p.42) – and the subtle problems of misperceptions of power – see *PR :: A problem of power* (p.47) – because all of these will impact every aspect of the enterprise. In each case, though, clarity on purpose is likely to provide the guiding star that's most needed to navigate through the dangerous shoals and stormy waters.

The same themes – or similar themes – also apply in other areas such as customer-relationship management, customer relationship training, work/life balance, product-personalisation and many others. All of these are about the links between people and work, or between people and the enterprise in general. There are plenty of tools and techniques to address these issues: use them.

Resources

🏛 Zachman framework: www.zifa.org

🏛 FEAF: www.cio.gov

🏛 TOGAF: see www.opengroup.org/architecture/togaf8-doc/arch/toc.html

🏛 Sally Bean, "The elusive enterprise architect", IT Adviser, Issue 43, May/June 2006;
www.nccmembership.co.uk/pooled/articles/BF_WEBART/view.asp?Q=BF_W EBART_205593

PA :: THE POLITICS OF PURPOSE

Principles

Whose work will be affected by any architectural strategy? In other words, who are the stakeholders in the architecture? And what will be their concerns with the architecture?

This is another one of those sections where in principle the issues should be simple and straightforward, yet in practice are usually anything *but* simple – because here is where we meet head-on with the tangled politics of change.

Fact is that architectural issues will *always* be emotive in some ways – see *DL :: Architecture is a feeling* (p.30). So it'll be best to start from an acceptance that it *is* fact, and design our activities accordingly – rather than trying to pretend it doesn't exist, and being caught out badly when it blows up in our faces.

The sources of the emotion are many and varied. Sometimes it's just that this is part of the 'bottom-up' response to our 'top-down' plan for architecture – see *DA :: The aims of architecture* (p.10). Sometimes it's from a general fear of change, which can be masked in many different ways – though more on this below. And sometimes it's because people can be passionately committed to their own local projects, and are understandably wary of anything that looks like an attempt at control from the centre. These last are people we need to treat with especial care and respect – see *KL :: A question of responsibility* (p.80) – because once we *do* get them on our side, they also become passionate advocates for the architecture itself.

> It was a *long* phone-call, at inter-state rates, but worth it in the end.
>
> They'd heard through the grapevine that we wanted a common solution for their own area of expertise, in quality-control and corrective-action. And they weren't happy about it. *Not* happy. *At all.*
>
> They'd worked on this for years, they said. Proven workflows. Proven results. Fully tested. No-one had done anything like it in any of the other states. Headquarters had never bothered to show any interest. So who the heck did we think we were, to come along and smash down all their work in favour of some half-baked ideas about

> architecture? I had to sit through what felt like an hour of angry ear-bashing in this vein before I finally had a chance to speak.
>
> All we'd done, I said, was that we'd used the architecture framework to identify what seemed to be a gap in the organisation's nationwide knowledge systems. And I'd been hoping to talk with them, as we'd heard they were one of the few groups in the whole organisation who were working in that space. Would they help us, I asked?
>
> Silence on the other end of the line. A long pause. Then: "Oh. Sorry." Another pause, and then, in a much brighter, happier tone: "Great! When can we meet?"

The polite euphemism for this delicate wrangling is that it's part of 'change management'. And although change management itself is often described as a linear process, from 'as-is' to a desired 'to-be' state, it's more realistic to think of it as cyclical, iterative, recursive, in the same way as the framework we're using here.

One of the most useful summaries of this human side of the change-process, and the ways we'll see the issues expressed in the comments we hear from stakeholders, is in the book *The Dance Of Change*, by Peter Sengé's 'Fifth Discipline' group. The issues change with the three phases of the change-cycle:

- the challenges of *initiating*:
  - not enough time: "we don't have time for this stuff!"
  - no help in coaching or support: "we have no help!", "we don't know what we're doing!"
  - a sense of a lack of relevance: "this stuff isn't relevant to us!"
  - a perceived difference between theory and practice: "they're not walking the talk!"
- the challenges of *sustaining*:
  - fear and anxiety: "this stuff is @#%#@!" (usually a mask for hidden fears such as "am I safe? am I adequate? can I trust others? or myself?")
  - assessment and measurement: "this stuff isn't working!"
  - perceptions about 'in-group' versus 'outsiders': "they don't understand us!", "we have the right way!", versus "I have no idea what they're doing!" or even "they're acting like a cult!"
- the challenges of *redesigning* and *rethinking*:
  - governance issues: "who's in charge of this stuff?" or "they won't give up the power!"

- diffusion and implementation of the architecture: "we keep reinventing the wheel!"
- full-circle, back to the starting-point with strategy and purpose: "where are we going?", "what are we here for?"

At some point, our architecture will need to address every one of these feelings and fears. It's never a quick process – nor ever an easy one. A great deal needs to be focussed on assisting people to find their own power and responsibility in relation to the architecture – see *PR :: A problem of power* (p.47) and *KL :: A question of responsibility* (p.80). But the first stage of that process is to identify as many as possible of the likely stakeholders, and their probable issues and concerns – and that's what we do here.

Procedure

Purpose

Identify change-management strategy required to address likely challenges to development and roll-out of whole-of-organisation enterprise-architecture.

People

Selected senior managers, strategists, enterprise architects, change managers, programme management office, others as appropriate.

Preparation

Standard business-analysis tools: whiteboard, meeting-space, pen and paper, time, and access to the required people.

Organisational directories, function-maps, etcetera; also social-network maps, Yellow Pages and similar narrative-knowledge tools, if available – see *PE :: What's the story?* (p.57).

Before you start, assess the architecture scope – see *DN :: Architecture of the enterprise* (p.13) – and maturity-level – see *MA :: Measuring maturity* (p.123).

Process

Using current scope and maturity-level as a guide, trawl through function-maps, organisational directories and, if available, organisational Yellow Pages or similar intranet contact-sites, to identify probable stakeholders – individuals or groups who may have concerns or need to be involved in the implementation of the current phase of architecture.

If social-network maps are available, identify relevant 'super-nodes' – people with large numbers of contacts, or focal-points for contact-trees – for potential stakeholders in the architectural space.

Where practicable, contact each of these stakeholders, and invite them to share their interests and concerns regarding the enterprise architecture. Assess any opportunities and risks that may arise from these discussions.

Record the stakeholder contact-list for use in future iterations, and document any identified issues. If appropriate, develop or amend a change-management strategy to address these issues.

Performance (artefacts and outcomes)

Stakeholder contact-list; opportunity/risk assessment; content for change-management strategy.

Broader applications

This perspective is *People / Appropriate* – an emphasis on the purpose-issues in relationships between people. Its direct counter-part is *Purpose / Elegant*, the 'people'-side of purpose – see *DL :: Architecture is a feeling* (p.30).

A clear sense of purpose is key here – see *DE :: Architecture on purpose* (p.21). Another is an awareness and acceptance that many of the clashes arise not because other people are being 'difficult', but because their work requires a different sense of *time*:

- *'purpose'-people* (strategists, futurists, senior executives): 'far future' – anything from five years to fifty years or more
- *'people'-people* (HR, marketers): near-random – from far past to far future
- *'preparation'-people* (planners, schedulers, project-managers): near future – hours, days, weeks, sometimes months
- *'process'-people* (production, delivery): immediate – an urgency of "*now!*"
- *'performance'-people* (accounts, analysts): past – last hour, last day, last week, month, quarter, financial-year

Respecting these differences in time-perspective, and translating cleanly between them, will go a long way towards easing many of the day-to-day political pressures in most aspects of organisations.

Again, Sengé's books – especially *Dance of Change* – are likely to be useful throughout the enterprise, especially at times when there's a need to grapple with the full complexities of change. It's not rocket-science, but it *is* emotive: the challenge is to prevent the waste of that energy in unnecessary in-fighting, and instead harness those emotions to propel the whole enterprise forward, for everyone's benefit.

Looking broader, it's useful to extend the same principles to all enterprise relationships: how well do each of these relationships fit with the enterprise purpose? Customer-value analysis can be useful here, likewise a stronger emphasis on use of principles and values to guide hiring-and-firing employment decisions. We can also apply the same principles to relationships with shareholders and other indirect stakeholders: we may well need investment from outside, but are these the right people to have that kind of hold over our business values and purpose. More controversial, certainly, but probably wise questions to ask...

Resources

📖 Peter M Sengé et al., *The Dance of Change: The challenges of sustaining momentum in learning organizations*, Currency (1999), ISBN-13 978-0385493223.

PR :: A PROBLEM OF POWER

Principles

What is the organisation's ability to do work?

This is another question that seems simple, and to which the answers should also be simple. But they're not. At all. In fact, it's the core of many of the issues that an enterprise-wide architecture aims to resolve.

Whilst a physics definition of 'power' would be 'the ability to do work', most *social* definitions of power are more like 'the ability to *avoid* work'. All too often, 'power' and authority seem to devolve from an ability to evade responsibility – see *KL :: A question of responsibility* (p.80) – and dump the difficult work onto others. Therein lies a *huge* problem for the practice of architecture, and for the architecture itself.

> We'd been warned about him – "a smug young know-it-all" was one of the politer epithets – but it was still one of those rare times when I almost lost my temper with a client...
>
> He'd summoned us to be shown his planned "New Way of Working" for the logistics division. We looked on aghast as he airily dismissed a thousand jobs, and another, and another – "all replaced by machines at half the cost", he said, with a salesman's certainty.
>
> We knew otherwise – knew just how unreliable and expensive in practice those machines really were – but that wasn't what worried me most. In addition to the human impact – of which he seemed blithely unaware – those front-line workers were also the main customer contacts; almost the only source of information for data-cleansing; the literal drivers for end-to-end quality-control. So yes, he'd done his financial analysis; but what about the impact on narrative-knowledge, on social-networks, customer-relations, morale and the rest? In other words, analysis of all the integration-issues that make the work possible – and on which the financial returns depend?
>
> "I don't need to do any of *that!*" he snapped. "The finance figures speak for themselves." His voice turned smarmy, sneering. "Besides, you don't have the authority. I have the ear of the board on this; I don't have to follow your architecture, *you* have to follow *me!*"

Here 'work', of course, is not just in the physical sense, but also mental, relational, all the other kinds of work that impact on all categories of the organisation's assets – see *KE :: Dimensions of architecture* (p.63). So what we need here is a systematic framework to identify any problem-areas which could limit the organisation's ability to do its desired work, and also the areas where things *are* going well, which we could leverage to improve capabilities elsewhere. The framework also needs metrics to monitor this 'ability to do work' – see *ML :: People and performance* (p.119).

Although any appropriate framework can be used, the one I prefer for this classifies power-issues into five distinct categories:

1: Actively dysfunctional – seen either as the win/lose "propping self up by putting other down", or the less-common lose/win style "putting self down to prop other up". Occasionally we'll even see this in IT designs, where improved efficiency for one system damages the efficiency of another. But a more common instance is where individuals or business-units are intentionally pitted against each other by a management with mistaken ideas about internal competition. The aim may be to improve overall sales, for example, but people soon discover it's easier to improve one's *relative* sales-figures by sabotaging others in the same team – with the result that everyone loses. These issues can easily become intractable, and very hard to resolve, especially as they're often surrounded by walls of denial and blame. As an architect, take great care when addressing any issue of this type.

2: Passively dysfunctional – this again has a win/lose form, "offloading responsibility onto others", and a less-common lose/win form, "taking on responsibility inappropriately from others". The simplest example is the 'silo' mentality – classic 'work to rule', 'demarcation disputes' and clumsy inter-system trade-offs – that we'll see in many poor system-designs, whether of organisational structures or IT-systems. Most early-maturity architecture is aimed at resolving IT-system issues of this type, and quietly addressing the related operational and governance issues that created the mess in the first place.

3: 'Best practice' – so-called because this is the best that can be achieved in a highly regulated environment. Active dysfunctions and silo-boundaries have been resolved, making it possible to create some level of cross-system and end-to-end integration – the main focus for mid-maturity enterprise-architecture. The limit here is the classic command-and-control mindset and its insistence on explicit cause and effect, making it impossible to cross over the boundary into complex-systems space – see the description of the Cynefin model in *KA :: Architecture as a way of thinking* (p.74).

4: Organisation supports individual variance – typified by self-adapting systems in both IT-based and human contexts, and also in issues such as ergonomics. In essence, the 'control' component of centralised command-and-control is eased in a partial shift from a rules-based to a principle-based model, devolving some decisions to the local level. The emphasis here is on the complex-domain, in Cynefin terms: enterprise-architecture needs a mid- to high-maturity level to support operations in this space, permitting a more pro-active and agile response, in conditions where events are only partially repeatable. In IT systems we'll see this, for example, as the more fluid relationships permitted by service-oriented architecture, and customised on-demand manufacture from a broad but pre-defined set of options.

5: Individual committed to organisation – known as 'wholeness responsibility' in human systems. This is what's required for the Cynefin 'chaotic' space, in which it's understood that nothing is ever truly repeatable, hence predefined rules are too misleading to be reliable in practice. This can only succeed via a fully principle-based model in which centralised 'command' is also dropped, devolving all run-time decision-making to the local level. To support this, the architecture must be at a high maturity-level, fully linking across all business dimensions – purpose, process, data, information, task and technology. This can rarely be sustained for long – at *some* point there will be a fall back to the previous level to redefine and re-assess principles, and refresh the sense of common identity – but is best supported by some kind of unifying focus-theme – see *TL :: The art of integration* (p.102).

Procedure

Purpose

Establish a framework to monitor 'ability to do work' across the enterprise and its partners, and to guide responses to issues identified in such monitoring.

People

Enterprise-architects, process architects, industrial psychologists, lead trainers, performance consultants; other stakeholders as appropriate.

Preparation

Standard business-analysis tools: whiteboard, meeting-space, pen and paper, time, and access to the required people.

Internet research on frameworks such as Human Synergistics' 'Life Styles Inventory' (LSI) or Tetradian's 'SEMPER'.

Stakeholder contact-lists, such as derived from section *PA :: The politics of purpose* (p.42).

Process

Using internet research, consultancy and other sources, identify candidate frameworks to assess 'ability to do work' across the scope covered by the current or intended enterprise-architecture.

Working with selected stakeholders, test and validate candidate frameworks. Select a framework which provides best fit for the architecture maturity-level and the organisation's culture.

Working with lead trainers and others as appropriate, develop a list of 'power' triggers and responses – in other words specific interventions to be applied in response to specific conditions of increasing or decreasing 'ability to do work' identified by the framework's metrics in specific domains covered by the scope of the enterprise-architecture.

Performance (artefacts and outcomes)

Whole-of-organisation metrics/diagnostics; list of trigger-values for metrics to link to response-framework.

Broader applications

This perspective is *People / Reliable* – an emphasis on anything that can make the actions of and interactions between people easier and more productive. Its direct counterpart is *Process / Elegant*, the use of an emotive 'theme' to drive process improvement – see *TL :: The art of integration* (p.102).

The power-dynamics described above are common to every aspect of every enterprise. No surprises there, I'd imagine, but it's worthwhile remembering to watch how they apply in practice in each area of work, and do what you can to lift the level in each case. Integrity / ethics training and monitoring can be useful here; likewise – as above – an explicit emphasis on identifying and maintaining win-win relationships with all the players and stakeholders in the enterprise.

Note that in the inherent uncertainty of the complex-domain – see 'Managing complexity' in *KA :: Architecture as a way of thinking* (p.74) – the one tactic that *doesn't* work is any attempt at rigid control: it invariably makes things worse. Instead, use the complexity tactic of 'probe / sense / respond': try out seed-ideas, seed-changes, watch carefully what happens, and use resonance – another principle from complexity-theory – to propagate the seeds that seem to work or suppress the ones that don't.

Resources

🏛 Human Synergistics' Life Styles Inventory: www.human-synergistics.com.au/content/products/diagnostics/lsi.asp

🏛 Tetradian SEMPER diagnostic: www.tetradian.com/semper

PN :: THE ROLE OF THE GENERALIST

Principles

Who are your generalists – the people who link *across* the different business domains? What support do they have in this role? And what support do they need?

This is another of these somewhat political aspects of enterprise-architecture. But at least it's less fraught than most we've seen so far, because the politics arise not from personalities but from the nature of organisations and their structures - which does take *some* of the heat out of the issue.

The political problem is straightforward, too. For good practical reasons, most organisations are structured and managed in vertical hierarchies; yet we also need a small number of people to operate horizontally *across* the hierarchies, to link all the vertical 'silos' into a single whole. Yet in doing so, they seem to break the ordered rule of the hierarchy. Most performance-metrics are vertical, and specialist – so the more these cross-functional, cross-domain generalists concentrate on their real work of horizontal linking, the less they appear to do. And by the nature of the work, generalists are often seen as disruptive: they ask awkward questions; make strange connections across 'silos'; blunder through jealously-guarded barriers of turf and territory; and generally waste other people's time by talking with them when they 'should be working'.

The result is that, all too often, this strange freedom of movement for a select few can be misunderstood as 'unfair' by people in ordinary specialist roles, or even as 'insubordination' by middle-level managers – with unfortunate results all round.

> It's clear they do *something*, but no-one really knows. In some cases all they seem to do is wander round and talk, though a few may hide away in a back-room somewhere, cooking up heaven-only-knows-what...
>
> To survive in large organisations, most generalists I know rely on blurry job-titles, vague job-descriptions, indefinite reporting-relationships. Groups might describe themselves as 'cross-functional teams', or as a 'skunk-works'. But it's harder for individuals to hide.

> One friend, in a major bank, was described as a lowly 'communications officer', although in reality she was the 'super-node' for the social-network that ran the bank's incident first-response system. Another, a foresight/strategy practitioner for a large pharmaceutical, had a business card with the impressive job-title of 'Ideation Manager'; but as he put it, "in this game, if you're not being fired at least once every two years, you're not doing your job properly!"

To protect themselves from zealous or vengeful inquiry, many generalists will hide behind a powerful patron. But useful as it is, this tactic can badly backfire: it leaves the generalists somewhat at the whim of the patron; and usually, when the patron moves on, the protection vanishes, which again can prove extremely uncomfortable, especially in environments with serious power-problems – see *PR :: A problem of power* (p.47). Far better, then to bring the generalists out into the open, by providing a better explanation of what it is they really do for the enterprise.

In essence, generalists work across the ordered/unordered boundary into the Cynefin 'complex' domain, in contrast to most people's roles in the ordered 'known' or 'knowable' domains – see 'Management of complexity' in *KA :: Architecture as a way of thinking* (p.74). Because the real world *is* complex and chaotic, in Cynefin terms, there'll always be a need for *someone* to prod, to probe, to run the strange experiments and seed-projects that allow the enterprise to sense and respond to the messy uncertainties and opportunities in its sphere of operations. By definition, then, these people *must* operate partly outside the rule-book; and also by definition, there are no simple metrics for what they do, because in the complex domain results can be measured only at the level of the whole, not in the performance of any single part.

Which brings us back to where we started: what do generalists *do*? Who would be a good generalist – rather than just a time-wasting dilettante? And how would we manage the generalists – their work, their performance?

Which bring us back, in turn, to enterprise-architecture, because by definition architects must in part be generalists: it's how they create connections across systems, be it low-level IT or the structure of the entire enterprise.

So we've covered some of this ground already – see *PL :: The architecture team* (p.34), for the overall attributes of generalists, the need to be a strong communicator, to learn fast, to build easy relationships with anyone, and so on. We'll also see other aspects in the management of tacit knowledge and social networks – see *PE ::*

What's the story? (p.57) - in responsibility-based ownership of assets – see *KL :: A question of responsibility* (p.80) – and in monitoring of complex performance – see *ML :: People and performance* (p.119). What we aim to add here are links to *other* generalists who we may need to add to the architecture as its maturity-level rises, or whose work *connects* with architecture rather than *is* architecture; and also to identify some means of measuring success of individual architects, and enterprise architecture as a whole.

Procedure

Purpose

Identify any additional cross-functional generalist roles required to implement enterprise-architecture, the required collective and individual skill-sets, and recommended collective and individual performance-criteria.

People

Selected senior managers, strategists, enterprise-architects, operations managers, lead trainers, HR specialists, performance specialists.

Preparation

Standard business-analysis tools: whiteboard, meeting-space, pen and paper, time, and access to the required people.

Stakeholder contact-lists, such as derived from section *PA :: The politics of purpose* (p.42).

Organisational directories, function-maps, etcetera; also social-network maps, Yellow Pages and other tacit-knowledge tools, if available – see *PE :: What's the story?* (p.57).

Before you start, assess the architecture scope – see *DN :: Architecture of the enterprise* (p.13) – and maturity-level – see *MA :: Measuring maturity* (p.123).

Process

Using the current scope and maturity-level as a guide for requirements, identify the *generalist* skills (cross-function, cross-technology, etcetera) and probable social-networks required for the implementation of the current phase of architecture. Conduct a gap-analysis against the skill-sets and social-networks of the existing members of the enterprise-architecture team and, if appropriates, candidates for the team.

Brainstorm potential performance-metrics and success-criteria, appropriate to the scope and complexity of the enterprise architecture. (At high maturity-levels, the scope will be the entire enterprise, and will be fully into the Cynefin complex-domain.) In particular, look for methods to identify complex-domain metrics, often based on what otherwise would *not* occur, such as cost-savings, opportunity-benefits and cross-system synergies.

Using the same requirements, trawl through the organisation's sources of role/contact information, such as function-maps, directories, social-network maps, and organisational Yellow Pages, to identify probable generalists whose work may intersect with the current or intended architecture phase, whose skill-sets or social-networks may complement those of the architecture-team, or who may otherwise be able to assist in rolling out the architecture.

Where practicable, contact each of these generalists, and invite them to discuss possible synergies and possible shared performance metrics. Assess any shared concerns, opportunities and risks that may arise from these discussions.

Record contact-lists, skill-sets, social-networks lists and performance criteria for use in future iterations, and document any identified issues. If appropriate, develop or amend a change-management strategy to address these issues.

Performance (artefacts and outcomes)

List of required skill-sets; content for cross-functional generalist job specifications and performance criteria; gap-analysis and change-management strategy for amendments to appropriate teams or units across the enterprise and/or its partners; content for architecture governance-charter and other enterprise-wide governance charters and reporting relationships.

Broader applications

This perspective is *People / Integrated* – an emphasis on the people-issues and people that help to pull the enterprise together into an integrated whole. The direct counterpart is *Performance / Elegant*, about the impact of these issues on overall performance – see *ML :: People and performance* (p.119).

The issues described in this section apply throughout the enterprise. The infamous 'org-chart' describes the vertical reporting structure, for example, but says almost nothing about how work is actually done, or how the separate 'silos' communicate with each other in order to complete any end-to-end process. Hence the need to understand the roles played by generalists, and any other horizontal mechanisms that link across the enterprise, and to provide them with such support – if often somewhat covert – that they may need.

It will also be relevant to cross-link any action here with other people-oriented concerns, such as the value of a unifying 'theme' such as a customer-centric model for service-structures – see *TL :: The art of integration* (p.102) – or support for creating a sense of 'wholeness responsibility' wherever practicable within the enterprise – see '5: Individual committed to organisation' in *PR :: A problem of power* (see p.47).

Resources

🏛 Tetradian SEMPER diagnostic: www.tetradian.com/semper

PE :: WHAT'S THE STORY?

Principles

From where or whom does the organisation's knowledge arise? Who identifies and creates business meaning? And how is this 'tacit knowledge' communicated, managed, refreshed, sustained?

From a knowledge perspective, many current 'enterprise architecture' frameworks such as Zachman, FEAF and TOGAF can be intensely frustrating, because they promote the delusion that knowledge is synonymous with IT. It isn't: in fact we could almost describe this as a kind of laziness, because although managing IT-based knowledge is rarely easy, managing the non-IT-based knowledge is *hard*.

> Over the decade we worked with them, we saw them go through the same pain and panic time after time – but still they wouldn't face the real source of the problem.
>
> Many of the major items handled by the unit went through the same cycle: major research when the item was first brought into service; a ten-, twenty-, thirty-year gap with only minor fixes needed; and then another major project to extend the item's working life. But after that gap, the senior people who'd worked on the initial projects were all either retired or dead – so there was no simple way to make sense of the previous work. Frequently all that was left was the final report – often much-modified for political reasons, and almost meaningless in practice – and an unedited, undocumented mess of source material. If they were lucky, there might also be some of the original test-journals and working-notes – though an official policy of discarding any material more than five years old often put paid to that. For one multi-million-dollar project, some sad staffer had to spend two *years* cataloguing the contents of forty filing-cabinets passed down through the decades – .and even that didn't help all that much.
>
> Nightmare: an *expensive* nightmare, repeated with every long-term project. Ouch.
>
> What they needed, to avoid that nightmare, was a systematic process to pass on the stories, the sensemaking, from one staffer to another, along with the source-material. But they wouldn't do it: instead, being technologists, they relied entirely on IT, which invariably went out of date within a decade – and in any case couldn't, and didn't, do the job.

At the end, what we need is business *meaning*. But we get there in three stages: content, context, and connections.

The *content* is just raw data: a photograph, a transaction, or the like. The more this information can be structured in some way, the easier it can be handled – hence the IT knowledge-infrastructure of databases, file-servers, on-screen forms and so on. The messier unstructured data tends to get left out of IT, however, simply because it's harder to handle. And hence, because it's not there with the rest of the data, a tendency to assume that it has no value – which can be a *big* mistake.

Without something to indicate the *context*, content can never be more than meaningless data – hence the increasing IT importance of metadata, 'information about information', such as date and time of a transaction, camera-settings and description for a photograph, and so on. Again, even though recent metadata models such as XML have extended the amount of 'unstructuredness' that can be managed in IT-based systems, there's still much of the messier metadata that gets missed out.

It's only when we make *connections* between information-items that we start to get close to *meaning*. The increasing sophistication in automated connections is almost a history of the past half-century of IT-systems: from structured records to entity-relationships, business-rules, object-models, business-intelligence, trend-analysis and 'fuzzy-pattern'-matching. But these still only work well with structured data and metadata: anything that doesn't fit will disappear from the picture. Which is a problem, for example, if we're trying to make sense of something which by definition doesn't exist – such as cost-savings, or opportunity-cost, or an un-planned-for external event.

The real difficulty, as Cynefin founder Dave Snowden put it, is that we know more than we can say, and can say more than we can write down. It's easy to share whatever's written down – hence the proliferation of IT-based 'knowledge management systems'. But what we really need is what people *know*. And that includes all the blurry, fuzzy, ifs-buts-and-perhaps, the subtle balance between big-picture and little-picture, without which we can make dangerously wrong connections – one famous example being the automated 'algorithmic trading' systems which triggered the stock-market crash of 1989.

In short, what we need are the *stories* – the 'narrative knowledge' of the enterprise. Stories are how people convey connections, and meaning – as 'the moral of the story', for example. The values of the enterprise – the ones we want, and the covert ones we don't –

are all conveyed by stories, all of which impact on the enterprise's 'ability to do work' – see *PR :: A problem of power* (p.47). And although people who work in controlled, known contexts learn best through 'best practice', maintenance-engineers and others dealing with inherent uncertainty share their knowledge through '*worst*-practice' – stories of what *didn't* work. Stories *matter*.

Stories, and most other forms of 'tacit knowledge', are also about people, and *in* people; so to manage this knowledge we also need to be more aware of people *as* people. Hence much of this kind of knowledge-management is about knowing who to ask, about passing the stories on, rewarding knowledge-sharing, and so on.

Yellow Pages directories, personal web-pages and weblogs, group wikis and communities-of-practice all help to create a culture of knowledge-sharing speeding searches for specialist knowledge. In the same way, responsibility-based ownership of information areas and business-rules – see *KL :: A question of responsibility* (p.80) – helps to break down delusions about knowledge and 'power', and safeguards transfer of knowledge when the responsibility changes hands, via exit-interviews and the like.

Another area of interest here is social-network mapping. Each link represents a connection between people – the owners of necessary knowledge. Clusters tend to form round two types of people: the key specialists, and the 'super-nodes'. Specialists maintain knowledge needed by many people; unless they're already overloaded, it's often useful to publicise that fact. By contrast, 'super-nodes' are usually generalists – see *PN :: The role of the generalist* (p.52) – who provide links across disparate groups and business functions; they may be even more important than the specialists, because they act as the 'glue' that holds the enterprise together.

Procedure

Purpose

Identify the scope and support for non-IT-based tacit knowledge, and key players or 'nodes' within the narrative-knowledge network.

People

Enterprise-architects and other generalists, knowledge-managers, lead trainers, HR specialists.

Preparation

Standard business-analysis tools: whiteboard, meeting-space, pen and paper, time, and access to the required people.

Internet research and other sources on narrative knowledge.

Organisational directories, function-maps, etcetera; also, if available, existing social-network maps and narrative-knowledge tools.

Social-network modelling tools – e.g. email-list scanners.

Process

In conjunction with knowledge-managers, use directories, social-network modelling tools and other sources to create architectural maps of tacit-knowledge capture, maintenance and exchange throughout the enterprise – including customers, partners and other 'outsiders' where appropriate.

Using the maps, identify potential leverage-points or requirements for system-change – either IT-based, such as Yellow Pages or specific weblogs; or process-based, such as communities-of-practice.

In conjunction with knowledge-managers and lead-trainers, identify requirements for training to improve tacit-knowledge capture, maintenance and exchange.

In conjunction with knowledge-managers and HR specialists, identify requirements for changes to performance-criteria, to reward knowledge-sharing and engagement in appropriate social-networks; and to HR procedures such as exit-interviews, to support tacit-knowledge retention and transfer.

Performance (artefacts and outcomes)

Social-network maps; Yellow Pages structures and equivalent access-frameworks for narrative knowledge; content for performance reviews and exit procedures.

Broader applications

This perspective is *People / Efficient* – an emphasis on the knowledge-aspects of people, particularly those which help to improve knowledge-sharing between people to improve collective efficiency. Its counterpart is *Preparation / Elegant*, the 'people'-aspects of knowledge, particularly around emotive commitments to shared knowledge – see *KL :: A question of responsibility* (p.80).

Narrative-knowledge is not specific to enterprise-architecture. The tendency to ignore non-IT-based knowledge, simply because it *isn't* IT-based, is a common enough in organisations, but the damage it can cause is incalculable, all the way up to disasters like the destruction of the *Challenger* space-shuttle. Although perceptions of 'knowledge management' may have slumped to the level of 'passé fad' in many places, the issues it deals with are still as urgent as ever. David Gurteen is one useful 'super-node' in the world-wide social-network for knowledge management: his Gurteen Knowledge Network website is worth exploring for ideas and contacts on how to address these issues in practice.

Such concerns are crucial where a context is highly regulated but the work itself is inherently uncertain: social-work casework is one example that comes to mind. In Cynefin terms – see 'Managing complexity' in *KA :: Architecture as a way of thinking* (p.74) - regulation is in the 'known' domain, but the main work of the case-worker is either in the expert 'knowable' domain, or over the boundary into the 'one-offs' of the complex domain: it's not an easy mix. Providing clarity on which framework applies at each moment – which parts of the work truly can be covered by laws, and which can only ever be guided by heuristics or principles – will make the work a lot less stressful for everyone, and also reduce the risk of inappropriate lawsuits.

Stories are also relevant in areas such as privacy management, reputation management, leadership, and social-market tactics used for market-development and market engagement – hence the thesis of the *Cluetrain Manifesto*, that 'markets are conversations'.

Resources

📖 Chris Collison and Geoff Parcell, *Learning To Fly: practical lessons from one of the world's leading knowledge companies*, Capstone, 2001; ISBN-13 978-184112509-1

📖 Etienne Wenger et al., *Communities of Practice: a guide to managing knowledge*, Harvard Business School Press, 2002, ISBN 1-57851-330-8.

📖 Peter M Sengé et al., *The Fifth Discipline Fieldbook: Strategies and tools for building a learning organization*, Currency (1994), ISBN-13 978-0385472562.

📖 David Gurteen and the Gurteen Knowledge Network: see www.gurteen.com

- 🕸 Large group interventions: see Martin Leith, www.largegroupinterventions.com/documents/leiths_guide_to_lgis.pdf
- 🕸 Social-network maps: see Wikipedia, en.wikipedia.org/wiki/Social_network , and Institute for Social Network Analysis of the Economy, www.isnae.org/sna.html
- 🕸 Anecdote: www.anecdote.com.au
- 🕸 Cynefin / Cognitive Edge: www.cognitive-edge.com
- 🕸 Cluetrain Manifesto: www.cluetrain.com

KE :: DIMENSIONS OF ARCHITECTURE

Principles

What information do you need, to identify and improve the effectiveness of the enterprise? What framework would you use to model this information?

The answers to these questions will depend in part on the scope and maturity of the enterprise-architecture – see *DN :: Architecture of the enterprise* (p.13) and *MA :: Measuring maturity* (p.123).

At an early-level maturity, the scope will usually be limited to sub-sections of IT, and the Zachman framework would be the most common guideline, though this comes more fully into its own at slightly higher maturity-levels.

For enterprise-wide IT-architecture, DyA or TOGAF would be used to complement Zachman; then FEAF or ARIS or ArchiMate, to link IT more strongly with process-models. Purpose-built modelling tools also become essential at higher maturity-levels, permitting multiple views into the same overall information.

But at the whole-of-enterprise level, with integration across every aspect of the enterprise, it becomes difficult not to drown in all that detail. To counter this, we need to go right back to core principles, further back even than basic notions such as the org-chart and the product-list, and start again with as clean a slate as we can. Anchoring the framework right up at that level gives us something to which we can link everything the enterprise is and does, as we work our way back down into the detail again.

Zachman's six categories – what, how, where, who, when, why – could work well as one such structure. In practice, though, it's now so enshrined as an IT-only framework that it's too probably confusing to use outside of that narrow scope. So an alternate approach I prefer is to think of the aspects of the enterprise not in terms of categories, but as *dimensions.*

To illustrate this, note that the enterprise is merely one player in an overall market. Watching what happens in a market, we can see four distinct yet interwoven dimensions to what's going on.

- Markets are *transactions*, traditionally about physical things, though less so in some areas of the market. Products are transferred from one player to another, and services are provided, on the basis of some notion of 'fair exchange' – price is one example, of course, but there are many others.
- Markets are *conversations* (to quote the *Cluetrain Manifesto*) – an exchange of ideas, opinions, experiences, which are sort of peripheral to a transaction rather than part of it.
- Markets are *relationships* – the transactions and conversations take place between people. Without those relationships – whatever form they may take – the market could not operate or exist.
- Markets are about identity and *purpose* – of individuals *as* individuals, and also shared purpose at various levels from single transactions to the market as a whole.

Hence four distinct dimensions, or types of assets: *physical*, or behavioural, in human terms, and also the physical 'things' of the enterprise; *conceptual*, or mental, the knowledge-assets each brings to the market; *relational*, or emotional, in part, including the relationships of each player in the market; and purpose, identity, morale, strategic business drivers and the like, forming the *aspirational* dimension – also traditionally be described as 'spiritual', though it's not a safe word to use in a business context.

The market is all of these things, all melded together in a kind of roiling mélange of *integration*, distinctive in its own right, which we might call the 'soul' of the market. Hence, in turn, the 'soul' of an enterprise. And it's *that* that we seek to model at the level of a whole-of-enterprise architecture.

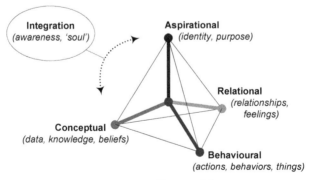

Tetradian model

Those four dimensions are linked together by bridging-themes such as vision and values, power and responsibility, leadership, narrative, active learning, sense-making and foresight. If we map all of dimensions and link-themes as a set of tetrahedral relationships, we have what I describe as a *tetradian*.

> In its bare form the tetradian looks a bit abstract, but with tweak or two it's a great tool to get business-people engaged in the architecture.
>
> For each of our new customers I would make up a customised version of the tetradian, using their own logo together with the descriptive labels on a small cardboard tetrahedron. It always got attention, because it made the architecture *tangible*: they could literally turn it over in their hands and see the whole from each different perspective.
>
> Then at one customer – a large logistics organisation – we found they were already using little icons to indicate process-types: gears to indicate machine-based processes, people beside a conveyor-belt for manual processes, and a computer-screen for IT-based ones. It matched the dimensions exactly. So for their version of the tetradian I took off almost all the words, and used their own icons instead.
>
> It worked beautifully. They were so popular that people started making their own copies; in days we found our little tetrahedrons popping up in all manner of unexpected places. It was an instant conversation-starter, making it much easier than usual to gain business buy-in.
>
> Is an icon worth a thousand words? No doubt at all in this case!

There's more on this on the Tetradian website, particularly the section on the SEMPER whole-of-organisation diagnostic. For many practical purposes, though, we need to lay the dimensions out into a flattened form. And for this, fortunately, there's a close map with the old Group Dynamics model of the project-cycle:

- 'Forming': the future-focussed initial phase of the project, outlining its *direction* and *purpose*
- 'Storming': the complex, almost beyond-time concerns of *people* and their *relationship* with each other
- 'Norming': settling out into the near-future focus of planning, the *knowledge* needed for *preparation*
- 'Performing': the urgent immediacy of the *physical*, of *process* and *practice*
- 'Adjourning': closure, completions, lessons-learned, measures of *performance*, the outcomes of *integration*.

Which gives us the core of the model we've used for this book:

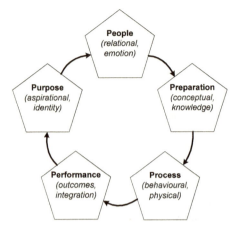

'Four-plus-one' dimensions and 5Ps framework

There's no doubt we need the lower-level detail models, such as functional models, business-system models, process-flow models, logical and physical-data models and all the rest. But by linking those models to a high-level framework of this type, we anchor them to the core of what the enterprise is and does.

Procedure

Purpose

Establish a framework for whole-of-organisation integration.

People

Enterprise-architects, strategists, other generalists.

Preparation

Standard business-analysis tools: whiteboard, meeting-space, pen and paper, time, and access to the required people.

Research on internet and other sources, for enterprise architecture frameworks and modelling toolsets.

Before you start, assess the architecture scope – see *DN :: Architecture of the enterprise* (p.13) – and maturity-level – see *MA :: Measuring maturity* (p.123).

Process

Using the current architecture scope and maturity-level as a guide, assess the suitability of each candidate framework to support the current and next phases of development of the enterprise architecture.

Also assess each framework for compatibility with the present or intended enterprise-architecture methodology and toolset – see *TR :: The practice of architecture* (p.96).

Where appropriate and practicable, identify and enter into the framework any initial content, using toolsets as available.

Publicise the selection of the framework and, if content has been entered, publish the framework with its initial content.

Performance (artefacts and outcomes)

Content and core structure for whole-of-enterprise architecture framework.

Broader applications

This perspective is *Preparation / Efficient* – a recursive emphasis on the overall knowledge needed to improve efficiency.

This isn't so much about types of thinking – those are explored more in *KA :: Architecture as a way of thinking* (p.73) – as the types of models and frameworks that can be used to guide that thinking, or to collate and categorise the appropriate forms of knowledge. The examples above are in the specific domains of enterprise architecture, but each industry and vertical domain has its own: ARIS, for example, is generally used in product development and production management, whilst others have been mentioned elsewhere – eTOM for the telecommunications industry, or SCOR for logistics. There are also many cross-industry frameworks: TQM, Six Sigma and the ISO9000-series standards for quality management, for example.

Look around, see what's available – there's plenty out there. The only catch is that most of them represent industry 'best practice', which is what we need in the Cynefin 'knowable' domain, the domain of the expert – see 'Managing complexity' in *KA :: Architecture as a way of thinking* (p.74) – but can be more of a hindrance when we move over to the boundary into the complex domain. In the inherent uncertainty of the latter, we need a framework that can handle '*worst*-practice', the kind of story-based knowledge by which case-workers and maintenance engineers share their knowledge – see *PE :: What's the story?* (p.57). Knowing which type of framework to apply in each context is an art-form in itself.

Another aspect of this perspective is that it's about the organisation's capability for innovation, for new thinking. Support for a systems-oriented view of the enterprise will be essential here: see, for example, Peter Sengé's *Fifth Discipline* books, and the section on 'Systems thinking' in *KA :: Architecture as a way of thinking* (p.75). Allocating explicit 'development time' or 'innovation time' in everyone's job description will also help here, though this often also needs a strong respect for inherent complexity – see 'Managing complexity' in *KA :: Architecture as a way of thinking* (p.74) in order for staff and their managers to understand the nature and value of 'failure' and, for that matter, of 'success'.

Resources

📖 Peter M Sengé, *The Fifth Discipline: The art and practice of the learning organization*, Currency (1990), ISBN-13 978-0385260954.

🏯 Zachman: www.zifa.com

🏯 DyA: eng.dya.info/Home/

🏯 TOGAF: see www.opengroup.org/architecture/togaf8-doc/arch/toc.html

🏯 FEAF: www.cio.gov

🏯 ARIS: www.ids-scheer.com/international/English/products/53961

🏯 ArchiMate: www.telin.nl/index?cfm.project=ArchiMate&language=en

🏯 Cluetrain Manifesto: www.cluetrain.com

🏯 Tetradian / SEMPER: www.tetradian.com/semper

KN :: AN EMPHASIS ON EFFECTIVENESS

Principles

What do we need to make the enterprise more effective?

If we ask business-people what they expect from enterprise archi-tecture, the most common answers are "increase efficiency" and "reduce costs". But it's quite easy to increase efficiency in one area by reducing the efficiency even more in others. And it's easy to reduce short-term costs, by destroying long-term capability. What matters most is not efficiency, but overall *effectiveness.*

For almost a century now, Frederick Taylor's theories of 'scientific management' have held sway, with their insistent – some would say obsessive – focus on efficiency and control. But in practice, as W Edwards Deming and others have demonstrated so well, Taylorism only works well for enterprises with stable products, stable processes, stable markets and rigidly-prescribed work-roles – which applies to very few of today's business contexts. For the rest, a focus on efficiency alone is a recipe for expensive disaster.

> There's a well-known example from when a large multi-national bought the consulting arm of another very large firm.
>
> The price had a terrifying number of zeroes after the currency-sign, but it had seemed such a great idea: 'a marriage made in heaven'. The consultants added great cachet to the company, and just the possibility of access to that dream-list of clients sent their salesmen salivating.
>
> But along came the company's bean-counters, who wanted "a few changes" in the name of efficiency. So gone were the consultants' coffee-machines; gone was any idea of personal workspace, replaced by 'cube-farm' hot-desks; gone even were any private rooms for meetings with clients. Oh, and performance was now to be measured solely on the number of boxes they sold — when none of them had ever sold anything in their working life. It was *not* a happy time...
>
> I happened to be visiting on the day everything went pear-shaped. Within weeks, *all* the consultants had left the new company, taking their clients with them — and there was nothing the company could do about it. All that remained from their huge investment was a name — and a few months later even that had faded into history.
>
> Very efficient, yes. But not very effective.

What we need is not just improved efficiency, but improvements in overall *effectiveness*. And no, it's *not* easy. But we can make it easier by being clear about what the components of effectiveness are. They map closely to the dimensions of the framework we're using here: Purpose, People, Preparation, Process, Performance:

- *Efficient* – optimise use of resources, and minimise waste. This comes from careful observation and re-planning, and fits well with the *Preparation* dimension. The observation and re-planning may be done by anyone appropriate – as in *kaizen* continuous improvement in TQM, for example.
- *Reliable* – timely, predictable, consistent, self-correcting. As might be expected, this corresponds with the *Process* dimension, especially in the physical domain.
- *Elegant* – clarity, simplicity, self-adjusting for human factors. Although this matches the *People* dimension, this is 'elegance' as much in the scientific sense – in other words clarity and the like, not for their own sake, but because it simplifies re-use, maintenance, adaptability, agility and pro-active response.
- *Appropriate* – supports and optimises support for business purpose. The *Purpose* dimension is essential to effectiveness, providing guidelines to allow activities to be 'on purpose'.
- *Integrated* – creates, supports and optimises synergy across all systems. This relates to the *Performance* dimension, because overall performance arises from a complex of outcomes which depend in turn on integration across all the functions of the enterprise.

Some applications of this checklist include:

- the overall 5Ps enterprise-architecture framework, to assess effectiveness across the entire enterprise and its interfaces with 'outside' agencies and organisations;
- the SCORE checklist in strategic assessment, to verify impact of strategy on overall effectiveness – see *TA :: What's the SCORE?* (p.106);
- structured feedback into the architecture, to improve the effectiveness of the architecture – see *ME :: Closing the loop* (p.116);
- implementations of Balanced Scorecard and other integrative metrics – see *MR :: Real-time scoreboards* (p.112).

Procedure

Purpose

Establish frameworks for assessment, review and measurement of cross-functional effectiveness.

People

Enterprise architects, strategists, process architects, knowledge managers, senior operations managers, lead trainers.

Preparation

Standard business-analysis tools: whiteboard, meeting-space, pen and paper, time, and access to the required people.

Research on internet and other sources, for methodologies on improving all aspects of effectiveness.

Assessments of existing capabilities and facilities for measuring and enhancing effectiveness at function and cross-function levels.

Process

Review existing methods for assessing effectiveness against the checklist above: efficient, reliable, elegant, appropriate, integrated.

Identify and document any changes required to improve effectiveness across the enterprise, and monitoring of effectiveness.

Outline change-requirements to amend performance metrics and training procedures accordingly.

Performance (artefacts and outcomes)

Metrics and content for cross-functional scorecards; content for cross-functional training and assessment procedures.

Broader applications

This perspective is *Preparation / Integrated* – an emphasis on how an awareness of the whole can be used to drive process improvement. Its direct counterpart is *Performance / Efficient*, on the ways in which shared knowledge can be used to pull the enterprise together – see *ME :: Closing the loop* (p.116).

The effectiveness-checklist above, and, in turn, this entire 5Ps framework, should apply not just to enterprise-architecture, but to every aspect of the organisation. All I can suggest here is: try it.

See what happens. Keep applying it recursively, iteratively, as a means to highlight potential for overall improvement.

Resources

✦ Tetradian SEMPER diagnostic: www.tetradian.com/semper

KA :: ARCHITECTURE AS A WAY OF THINKING

Principles

What principles and frameworks will you use to guide your own thinking about the enterprise-architecture?

For the most part this choice depends on the business drivers. If the key concern, for example, is simply to reduce the direct cost of IT systems, the conventional domain-specific approach of FEAF or TOGAF will do the job.

But as architectural maturity develops, the business drivers move into complex territory: greater agility, process re-use, customer-centric customisation, shared end-to-end processes, self-adapting systems, and so on. As scope broadens, andtime-horizons move both further away (for strategy) and closer (for time-to-market), the approach we need becomes more and more abstract. Yet at the same time it still has to make sense for people who aren't at all comfortable with abstracts. Therein lie some real challenges for enterprise-architects.

> In our first attempt to show the true value of that logistics early-warning system, we made the mistake of showing the process-flows in the form of a Business Process Modelling Notation diagram. BPMN is great for the formal modelling rigour needed by software engineers, but *not* for a board-level presentation: the blank stares and silence from round the table sent us away in shame.
>
> For the next meeting, we redrew the diagram, with the exact same process-flows, but replacing the bland BPMN boxes with clip-art pictures of trucks, conveyor-belts, fork-lifts, sorting-machines, delivery staff. This time it clearly made sense: we gained our go-ahead.
>
> These senior people weren't 'stupid': when we explained it in their own terms, they understood straight away. The problem before was that they didn't have time to learn an abstract language and translate it back into their concrete world. As architects, we did need that level of abstraction: but it was also our responsibility to each audience to do the translation from the abstract into the everyday.

The requirement here, then, is to identify and document the frameworks to be used, the audiences to which each will apply, and the translations between them.

Business drivers

The first requirement is a clear grasp of the *business drivers* for the enterprise: its goals, its objectives, its purpose. These need to be defined in architectural rather than marketing terms: more on this in the section *DE :: Architecture on purpose* (p.21). This provides the context in which to interpret basic-level business needs to reduce system costs, complexity and the like.

At the next level of maturity, the most common requirement is consolidation and *re-use*, through design principles such as identification of system patterns, and through a service-oriented architecture – see *KR :: The centrality of services* (p.84)

The next level aims for improved enterprise *agility*. In an iterative agile development methodology, the limits for each iteration are time and budget, not features, and system requirements need to be prioritised with care – see *TE :: Requirements for agility* (p.89).

At each level, the business is likely to call for ever-increasing efficiencies. However, the real concern is not efficiency, but overall *effectiveness*, of which efficiency is only one component – see *KN :: An emphasis on effectiveness* (p.69).

Managing complexity

Many of the contexts and issues that architects will need to deal with have *inherent complexity*. These are often identified as 'intractable problems', which seem at first to respond to conventional attempts at control, but fall back into problematic conditions time after time. Culture and quality-management are two common examples.

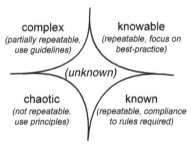

Cynefin model of context complexity

The Cynefin model above describes what's going on. At first, everything is in that central region of the 'unknown' – labelled 'disorder' in the original model, which is slightly misleading here.

We then have four distinct ways to make sense of this 'unknown': assume that it is known; find some way to make it knowable; accept its inherent complexity; or accept it as an unrepeatable 'market of one'.

Most businesses – especially those in a high-compliance context, such as banking or medicine – would prefer to force all processes into the 'known' domain of explicit controls; yet often the best that can be achieved is 'knowable', the domain of best-practice and expert analysis. But the complex domain is *qualitatively* different: any apparent pattern of cause-and-effect can only be identified retrospectively, requiring tactics that Dave Snowden, the original developer of Cynefin, describes as 'probe / sense / respond', rather than 'sense / analyse / respond' as in the 'knowable' domain. Cynefin is one of the most useful models for sense-making in the complex domain; you'll find more details at the Cognitive Edge website.

One of the main methods to 'probe' into the complex domain is through *narrative inquiry*, exploring the tacit knowledge of the enterprise via stories and anecdotes – see *PE :: What's the story?* (p.57). There's more information on this at the Cognitive Edge website, and also at the Australia-based Anecdote website.

Narrative inquiry is also an important tactic for tackling the non-repeatable *'chaotic' domain* – contexts such as unique customisation ('market-of-one'), and one-off development and maintenance. For example, many engineers learn not through best-practice, but *worst*-practice – stories of what *didn't* work as much as what did.

Systems thinking

Perhaps *the* essential in the enterprise-architect's toolkit is an ability to view the whole of a context *as* a whole, and as *systems of systems*. For my own architecture work, I usually model the highest level of systems as a set of *dimensions* – see *KE :: Dimensions of architecture* (p.63) – which map, for example, to everyday business concerns such as transactions, relations, conversations, business purpose and overall integration.

Systems thinking is also the core skill described by Peter Sengé and his colleagues in their books on the concept and practice of the 'learning organisation' – *The Fifth Discipline, The Fifth Discipline Fieldbook* and *The Dance of Change*. Although systems-theory can be dauntingly complex, the essentials for architecture can be summarised by five key concepts.

The first is *rotation* – a systematic process of assessing a context from multiple perspectives. The methodology described in this book is a kind of rotation through different views on the role and practice of enterprise-architecture.

Next is *recursion*, a 'nesting' of a pattern within the same kind of pattern - of which one of the most common forms is the hierarchical structure of the everyday 'org-chart'. These are patterns of relationship or interaction which repeat or are 'self-similar' at different scales: identifying such recursion can make it possible to reduce complex-seeming processes into a simple set of patterns.

Another systems concept is *reciprocation* – the understanding that, with one key exception, systems must always balance out somehow. What makes it difficult to analyse is that this reciprocal balance is not necessarily direct or immediate. In many cases balance may only be achieved over time at a system-wide level, with 'energy-transfers' often occurring between the dimensions – a classic example being a 'slash and burn' tactic which gives a short-term financial gain, but balances out by destroying the organisation's ability to do work, wiping out all of the supposed gains over a longer period of time.

The exception to that reciprocal balance is the result of *resonance* – the feedback-loops which can be found in all complex real-world systems. In systems-theory this can occur through 'positive feedback' or feedforward – both of which increase the 'snowball effect' towards self-propagation – or as 'negative feedback', or damping, which reduces the effect.

The last concept, *reflexion*, is also perhaps the strangest aspect of systems-theory. It's a corollary of recursion, in that the whole, or aspects of the whole, can be identified within the attributes and transactions of any part at any scale. Everything is connected to everything else – is *part of* everything else. A useful analogy here is a hologram: unlike an ordinary photograph, even the tiniest fragment of a true hologram will contain a complete picture of the whole, if only in limited detail. The same is true of business systems: once we develop an eye for reflexion, and see how it works in practice, we can start anywhere, in any appropriate part of the system, and leverage the results out into the whole.

The mindset of the architecture team

You'll find more details on the mindset and skill-sets of the architecture team in the section *PL :: The architecture team* (p.34).

Enterprise architects also need to be disciplined generalists – see *PN :: The role of the generalist* (p.52).

Procedure

Purpose

Identify the key frameworks and theoretical models that will be used to guide enterprise-architecture principles and practice.

People

Selected senior managers, strategists, enterprise-architects, knowledge managers, lead trainers.

Preparation

Standard business-analysis tools: whiteboard, meeting-space, pen and paper, time, and access to the required people.

Internet and other research for frameworks, models and other sources of information.

Assess the maturity-level of the present architecture before you start – see *MA :: Measuring maturity* (p.123).

Process

Starting with the material gleaned from the internet or other research, use brainstorming and other group facilitation techniques with the selected key stakeholders to identify ideas, models and frameworks which 'make sense' at the current maturity-level and for the specific context.

Note that the models and frameworks to be used for training and in published materials may well need to vary according to audience-group. For example:

- IT-centric frameworks such as Zachman, FEAF and TOGAF will always provide useful guidelines for IT staff.
  However, in their standard form they will rarely make sense to others: for those, use only a small business-oriented subset such as a functional business model and business-system model.

- Systems-theory, complexity-theory and the like will rarely make sense in production environments. Most people do not have *time* to think in abstracts: they need explicit guidance for quick decisions on how to act or escalate. At higher maturity-levels for architecture, systems-theory models will be valuable for all staff, but should be reserved for use in pre- and post-action reviews away from the production environment.

Document the decisions, the sources and the respective audience-groups.

Performance (artefacts and outcomes)

List of reference sources; content for training manuals.

Broader applications

This perspective is *Preparation / Appropriate* – an emphasis on selecting frameworks, mental-models and mindsets that support the purpose of the enterprise. Its direct counterpart is *Purpose / Efficient*, about ways to describe that purpose – see *DE :: Architecture on purpose* (p.21).

The focus here is on a 'knowledge audit' of methods of thinking that provide clarity on purpose, and how those methods feed back (or forward) into practice. Brainstorming, analogy, metaphor, stories and all manner of 'idea generators' could apply here; likewise futurist or foresight techniques in general.

The notes above about systems-thinking and the like also apply to the broader enterprise. And Peter Sengé's *Fifth Discipline* books, for example, are even more relevant to the general day-to-day business environment than to enterprise-architecture.

Another likely area of interest is the work by Christopher Alexander and others on 'patterns', an abstract template or building-block for some aspect of an enterprise. Alexander's original work – published as *"A Pattern Language"* – was on physical architecture and buildings, but the same principles apply to many other areas of direct relevance to business: software patterns, process patterns and workflow patterns, to name a few. Well worth exploring.

Resources

⟐ Zachman: www.zifa.org
⟐ FEAF: www.cio.gov

- TOGAF: see www.opengroup.org/architecture/togaf8-doc/arch/toc.html
- ARIS: www.ids-scheer.com/international/English/products/53961
- DyA: eng.dya.info/Home/
- VSM: see en.wikipedia.org/wiki/Viable_System_Model
- Complexity: see Cynefin / Cognitive Edge, www.cognitive-edge.com
- Narrative knowledge: see Anecdote, www.anecdote.com.au
- Fifth Discipline (five disciplines): www.fieldbook.com/mainfiveDs.html
- Idea-generators – see www.ideaflow.com/ideagen.htm
- Futurist and foresight techniques – see Association of Professional Futurists, www.profuturists.org

- Christopher Alexander, *A Pattern Language: towns, buildings, construction*, Oxford University Press, 1977, ISBN 0195019199.
- Peter M Sengé, *The Fifth Discipline: The art and practice of the learning organization*, Currency (1990), ISBN-13 978-0385260954.
- Peter M Sengé et al., *The Fifth Discipline Fieldbook: Strategies and tools for building a learning organization*, Currency (1994), ISBN-13 978-0385472562.
- Peter M Sengé et al., *The Dance of Change: The challenges of sustaining momentum in learning organizations*, Currency (1999), ISBN-13 978-0385493223.

KL :: A QUESTION OF RESPONSIBILITY

Principles

Who's responsible for each of the enterprise's knowledge-assets? What are these assets? How are the responsibilities identified, supported, maintained and transferred?

These questions focus on responsibility-based 'ownership' of non-tangible assets – all those assets that are based more in people than in systems or physical 'things'. Whilst the principle of such ownership is well understood for specific domains – the concept of 'project owner', 'data owner', 'business-rule owner' and so on – our architecture needs to address it in a broader and more consistent way. In effect, we need an architecture of responsibility.

This is important, because responsibility drives organisational agility – see *TE :: Requirements for agility* (p.89). As an expression of trust, in both directions, it also tends to lift the functionality of the power-dynamics – see *PR :: A problem of power* (p.47).

> "When I want your opinion, I'll give it to you! So shut up and do what you're told!"
>
> That's an exact quote from a manager to a staffer, during one of the more difficult assignments undertaken by a colleague of ours. As a consultant, she'd been asked to find a way to improve a seriously dysfunctional – and seriously loss-making – business-unit in a large enterprise. Commitment and responsibility are essential to success, but blame-based cultures like that one are characterised by a systematic *evasion* of responsibility – making success hard to attain.
>
> Harder still is that in some environments, people are actually penalised for taking responsibility: "no good deed goes unpunished" is one ironic catch-phrase we've heard all too often. It's hard to improve anything when it's not safe to do your own work well...
>
> It *is* possible to resolve that kind of mess. After eight months of hard work, our colleague had brought that unit back from the brink, to the point where it was even making a modest profit. The core of it, she said, was about creating conditions in which people could find their own responsibility and pride – and keeping the blamers at bay.

There's a strong link between responsibility and the knowledge-management issues around tacit knowledge in general – see *PE ::*

What's the story? (p.57) – not only because the maintenance and sharing of narrative-knowledge depends on personal responsibility, but because we will often need to publish contact-details for asset-owners in a Yellow Pages intranet or something of that kind.

Responsibility is emotive – a *personal* commitment to the maintenance of the asset. As a result, it's often linked to the enterprise values, and to more subtle assets such as shared morale – see *DL :: Architecture is a feeling* (p.30) and *PA :: The politics of purpose* (p.42). And individuals are more likely to develop that commitment if they feel they can connect with the purpose of the enterprise – see *DE :: Architecture on purpose* (p.21).

The *active* acceptance of responsibility is always the result of personal choice. Despite job-descriptions and the like, responsibility for non-tangible assets cannot be assigned, and certainly cannot be imposed or enforced, because there is no identifiable action or physical 'thing' that can be traced. Any kind of force will eventually lead to the loss of the asset. Instead, we need to provide conditions under which individuals can assume, adopt, embrace the required responsibilities.

The core issue is one of *trust*, a sense of safety in both directions. At the same time, the enterprise needs to ensure that the asset is shared appropriately, on a 'need to know/need to use' basis. Identity-management and human security are valid concerns here.

Transfer of responsibility from one person to another is a transfer of trust – with all the subtle complications this implies. Long-term knowledge-management, for example, often requires a transfer of tacit knowledge from one generation to another, even though that generation may never use the knowledge itself. If this transfer fails at any stage, the knowledge can rarely be retrieved – as illustrated in the example in *PE :: What's the story?* (p.57). This becomes a significant issue in risk-assessment and risk-management.

For the same reason, exit-interviews and similar HR processes are essential to capture tacit knowledge that could otherwise be lost. Such processes need to be identified and modelled as an explicit part of the enterprise's knowledge architecture.

Procedure

Purpose

Establish framework for responsibility-based 'ownership' of core non-tangible assets.

People

Enterprise architects, knowledge managers, HR specialists, security specialists.

Preparation

Standard business-analysis tools: whiteboard, meeting-space, pen and paper, time, and access to the required people.

Assessments of existing capabilities and facilities to support responsibility-based ownership of non-tangible assets.

Research on internet and other sources, for strategies, tactics, techniques and methodologies to create and maintain responsibility-based ownership.

Process

Together with knowledge-managers, review existing capabilities to identify, promote and support responsibility-based ownership of tacit knowledge-assets.

With knowledge-managers and HR specialists, review existing processes for transfer of responsibility-based ownership of knowledge-assets and other responsibilities.

With knowledge-managers and security specialists, review existing processes for management of responsibilities, identity-management and 'need to know/need to use' access to tacit knowledge-assets, and other security risks and opportunities arising from responsibility-based ownership of knowledge-assets.

Identify and document any changes required to improve management and operation of responsibility-based ownership of knowledge assets across the enterprise.

Outline change-requirements to amend processes, systems, metrics and training procedures accordingly.

Performance (artefacts and outcomes)

Repository for 'ownership' responsibilities; content for information security procedures and processes; content for related HR procedures such as exit-interviews.

Broader applications

This perspective is *Preparation / Elegant* – an emphasis on the 'people'-aspects of knowledge and process-improvement, particularly around emotive commitments to shared knowledge. Its counterpart is *People / Efficient*, about the knowledge that resides *in* people – see *PE :: What's the story?* (p.57). Each of these provide different views on the same issues of 'tacit knowledge' – the non-IT-based knowledge through which business-meaning is derived.

The descriptions above for enterprise-architecture also apply to every other aspect of the enterprise, its work, its processes and its knowledge. The procedure in each area would be much the same as above: in the 'People' section for the procedure, add the appropriate domain-experts for the area, with the purpose, preparation, process and performance-artefacts of the procedure remaining the same.

An ideal outcome of the procedure would be a 'Yellow Pages'-style repository and directory of ownership-responsibilities that covers every aspect of the enterprise, making it easier not only to identify key responsibilities, but to accelerate knowledge-sharing. The catch is that this isn't a fit-and-forget exercise – it needs to be maintained by a culture of knowledge-sharing, underpinned by an appropriate set of HR processes. Collison and Parcell's book *"Learning To Fly"* shows some detailed examples of how this type of knowledge-management works in practice.

Resources

📖 Transfer of trust: David Maister et al., *The Trusted Advisor*, Free Press, 2002, ISBN 0743207769

📖 Chris Collison and Geoff Parcell, *Learning To Fly: practical lessons from one of the world's leading knowledge companies,* Capstone, 2001; ISBN-13 978-184112509-1

🏯 SEMPER diagnostic: www.tetradian.com/semper

KR :: THE CENTRALITY OF SERVICES

Principles

What services are described in the architecture of the enterprise? What interfaces do these services expose? How are these interfaces published? Who or what are the consumers of these services? And how do service-levels change with varying implementations of each service?

Service-oriented architectures are increasingly common in designs for IT-systems. By describing relationships between systems in a consistent way, as 'services', IT complexity can be greatly reduced. But here, as indicated by the last question above, we're exploring a larger picture than just the enterprise's IT: at this level, we describe *everything* the enterprise does in terms of services.

In effect, every business-process is a self-contained system that provides a service. And each of these services needs clear service contracts with its 'providers' and 'consumers', with explicit Service Level Agreements (SLAs), Key Performance Indicators (KPIs), Key Success Criteria (KSCs) and the rest.

In this sense, a systems view of services and service-oriented architecture is a key to creating simplicity across the whole enterprise – and all of the business benefits that that would bring.

It's important to understand services first in this abstract way, because it tells us the nature of each service, and what service-contracts are required with its providers and consumers, independent of how the service is implemented.

> "A service is comprised of manual processes, [physical technology such as] logistics equipment, and information systems..."
>
> This extended concept of services is based on work done by the business-transformation team at one of our clients, who'd mapped their processes and systems in terms of those three dimensions above. These were indicated on their business-systems models by three little icons: people beside a conveyor-belt, for manual processes; a set of gears, for physical machinery; and a computer-screen, for IT.

What I've done here is to extend that concept to include the business dimension, and to link it more strongly with systems-theory – of which more below – but the original idea was theirs.
Fair's fair: credit where credit's due!

With this broader understanding of the nature of the service, we can *then* choose what mix of IT, manual people-processes and machine-technology to use in each implementation.

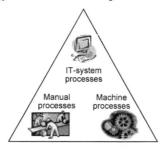

A service is any combination of IT, people and machines

There's an analogy here with the classic Soil Types diagram, familiar to farmers and gardeners. Each type of soil is a mix of different amounts of clay, sand and silt. There's no one 'best' soil, though there's an optimum range for any given purpose. The same is true for business-services: there's usually an optimum mix of IT, people and technology, but in principle almost any mix could work.

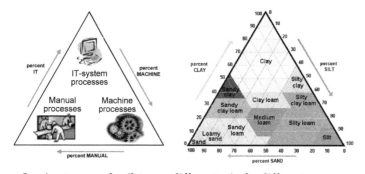

Service-types and soil-types: different mix for different purpose

Each different mix will give the service different SLAs, and different internal processes. But the *overall* service – the published interfaces, the external service-contracts, the KPIs and KSCs – should remain the same. Among other advantages, this simplifies planning for overload and for disaster-recovery: we can change the service implementation – the mix of IT, people and technology – without changing the nature of the service itself.

These three dimensions cover only the operations space. To cover all aspects of the enterprise, we'd also need to include the business dimension of 'purpose'. For that, we'd need to map the mix as a tetrahedron rather than a triangle – see *KE :: Dimensions of architecture* (p.63) – but otherwise the principle is exactly the same.

The design, implementation and improvement of services must be driven by clear and explicit requirements – see *TE :: Requirements for agility* (p.89) – and managed through an appropriate framework – see *TN :: Managing services* (p.93).

In many systems-theory frameworks, living organisms are modelled as sets of interacting, mutually-supportive services. This approach provides valuable insights for modelling enterprise-level services as a 'living organisation'. For example, Stafford Beer's 'Viable System Model' provides a gap-analysis checklist for service completeness:

- what is the service's *purpose*? who or what defines *policy*?
- what is the current *strategy*? outside *relationships*? who defines this?
- how are the service's *tasks defined, managed and monitored*?
- what *random checks and audits* are used to *verify performance*?
- how is the service *coordinated* with other services?
- what does the service *do*? how does it support its 'downline' services (if any)?
- how does the service identify and resolve any *run-time exceptions*?
- what *corrective-action* does the service undertake for causes of issues?
- how does the service *track* and *manage quality-issues* and other issues?
- how does the service manage *improvement* of its *processes*?

Although service-oriented architectures do require considerable effort to define, design and implement, the returns in simplicity and agility are well worth the investment.

Procedure

Purpose

Establish framework for a high-level service-oriented architecture, including design, implementation and review of cross-functional or inter-functional services and their interfaces.

People

Enterprise architects, IT architects, process architects, business-continuity specialists.

Preparation

Standard business-analysis tools: whiteboard, meeting-space, pen and paper, time, and access to the required people.

Assessments of existing service capabilities and models, and of the architecture scope – see *DN :: Architecture of the enterprise* (p.13).

Research on internet and other sources, for service-oriented architectures and their implementations.

Process

In conjunction with the full team above, assess services within the current and intended architecture scope. Identify the 'providers' and 'consumers' of each service, and the implied or actual service-contracts, SLAs, KPIs and KSCs.

Using frameworks such as FEAF's Service Reference Model and the Viable System Model, evaluate services for completeness and identify potential to simplify, streamline or cluster services into hierarchies.

As appropriate, brainstorm alternate implementations of services under different scenarios, such as for process improvement, process reengineering or disaster-recovery. Ensure that the interfaces, KPIs and KSCs remain the same in each implementation.

Document results as recommendations or requirements for future change.

Performance (artefacts and outcomes)

Service reference-models, process models, high-level service interface specifications; content for business-continuity procedures.

Broader applications

This perspective is *Preparation / Reliable* – an emphasis on the practicality of knowledge, and frameworks to verify its completeness and usefulness. The counterpart is *Process / Efficient*, about preparation and knowledge to underpin day-to-day practice – see *TE :: Requirements for agility* (p.89).

The same principles above should apply throughout the entire enterprise. Here we've concentrated on services as one type of framework, but there are many others – the real concern is not the framework itself as the methods used to verify completeness.

Checklists are the obvious tools for this, of which the Viable Systems Model checklist above is one such example that could be used in many other contexts besides services. Cyclical structures – such as TQM's 'plan, do, check, act' sequence, or the Group Dynamics 'forming, storming, norming, performing, adjourning' cycle that underlies this 5Ps framework – are useful here too, as the structure provides both a checklist and a guiding framework for action. Other tools include knowledge-audits and knowledge management reviews, and integrated performance support systems (IPSS). Just remember, as you apply these tools to any work-environment, that the tool itself doesn't matter: it's how the tool can be used to improve reliability, consistency, the overall process, that is the real emphasis here.

Resources

- FEAF Service Reference Model: see
  www.whitehouse.gov/omb/egov/a-2-EAModelsNEW2.html
- Viable System Model: for links and references, see
  en.wikipedia.org/wiki/Viable_System_Model

TE :: REQUIREMENTS FOR AGILITY

Principles

What requirements and other information-items are needed, to drive enterprise agility? How are they collected, collated, monitored, maintained, reviewed, re-used?

Agility is the aim, but the means to identify what that agility *is*, what it's for, what the results should look like, and how to get there, are all dependent on appropriate documentation of requirements. Every decision is a requirement, from the most minor detail such as the colour of an item on a screen, all the way up to the enterprise Vision – see *DE :: Architecture on purpose* (p.21). So we need some means to gather these requirements, collate them, cross-reference them and so on; and somewhere to store them so that they're available as needed.

This applies not just to projects, but to the architecture itself. The common notion of an 'as-is' architecture versus a single 'to-be' future-state is a close analogy to the classic Waterfall development model: the requirements may seem technically correct, perhaps, but the whole process is too cumbersome to be useful. Instead, as in Agile development models such as DSDM, we turn the process on its head: not allocate time and budget to fit the requirements, and wait, and wait, and wait – as in Waterfall – but set the time and budget, and prioritise the requirements to fit.

> This book itself illustrates the difference between the two models. Conventional book production is like Waterfall. We start with an idea, develop an outline, flesh out the detail and so on – in other words, define the book's requirements. We only get one shot at this, so immense care is needed to decide what's in and what's out. Then we develop the content, send it back and forth to reviewers, because it has to be perfect before it goes to press. The editorial process alone can take months, years even. And we have to print at least a thousand copies to cover all those costs – and pray we don't end up with a pile of unsold stock because the book's already out of date.
>
> By contrast, in an Agile approach, we set the time-budget, and trim the requirements accordingly. In this case, I've set myself a limit of two months from start to finish, to write not 'the book', but a *first iteration*

of the book. I don't aim – and don't *need* to aim – for an impossible
'perfection': instead, the emphasis is on 'just enough, just in time', to
get the ideas out there and in everyday use as fast as possible. We use
e-book production and print-on-demand technology to bypass most of
the start-up costs of conventional print, making it almost as economic
to print one copy as a thousand. And the peer-review happens *after*
production, testing and validating each idea in practice, and collating
the results as requirements for a new iteration, with an update
available in weeks, maybe even in days.

Which approach is better? Depends on your requirements, really…
but if time-to-market is important, Agile is the only way to go.

One reason why Waterfall so often leads to monolithic failures is
that we never *do* get 'the right requirements' it needs. Waterfall
requires everything to be written down in advance: yet the reality
is that people know more than they can say, and can say more
than they can write down – see *PE :: What's the story?* (p.57). There
are always nuances, twists, uncertainties, if-buts-and-perhapses
that are often cleaned out in the review process, but turn out to be
extremely important in practice; and those few people who *are*
certain of anything usually turn out to be wrong anyway.

Instead, Agile makes it possible to say "I don't know what I want,
but I'll know it when I see it", and work out the detail of requirements as we go along. This iterative approach also feeds into the
'plan, do, check, act' cycle of Total Quality Management – the
'active learning' that underpins process revision and review.

Requirements-gathering is similar in all approaches, but requirement priorities become even more important in Agile, because
they guide choices for iterations, and change dynamically with
each iteration. One common prioritisation style is referred to as
'MoSCoW':

- **M**ust have – essential
- **S**hould have – preferred
- **C**ould have – desirable
- can **W**ait till next iteration

There are also relative dependencies to take into account: something may have a high priority, but only becomes implementable
when something else is available to support it. To give an example
from a current project, we need a link to the Justice Department
system, but can only build it when their interface schema is ready,
and our own enterprise-service-bus implemented, both of which
may be several months away. We need to define work-arounds for
unimplemented requirements, especially the high-priority ones –

and those work-arounds need to be dropped when the real system comes on-line.

So the requirements process must reflect all these needs. Many practitioners use the Rational framework, but my experience is that it's only well suited for software development. I prefer the Robertsons' 'Volere' methodology, which I've used for years, and is also recommended in the TOGAF ADM – see the Volere website for more details. The Volere website also includes an extensive listing of requirements-repository toolsets and applications.

Procedure

Purpose

Establish a methodology and cross-functional repository for dynamic business-system requirements.

People

Enterprise architects, senior business analysts, programme management office.

Preparation

Standard business-analysis tools: whiteboard, meeting-space, pen and paper, time, and access to the required people.

Research on internet and other sources, for requirements methodologies and toolsets.

Process

In conjunction with analysts and the PMO, identify requirements for the requirements methodology and repository, including access, security, version-control and related issues.

Document the results as recommendations or requirements for implementation or future process change.

Performance (artefacts and outcomes)

Requirements repository; content for procedures on use and governance of requirements repository.

Broader applications

This perspective is *Process / Efficient* – an emphasis on preparation and knowledge to underpin day-to-day practice. Its counterpart is *Preparation / Reliable*, about the practicality, completeness and usefulness of knowledge – see *KR :: The centrality of services* (p.84).

For more general applications, part of this perspective would include the supply-chain analysis and classic Taylorist collating of information for process improvement or process reengineering, though preferably with more awareness of the importance of knowledge from the field-workers – as in active-learning and *kaizen* TQM – see *ME :: Closing the loop* (p.116) – and also over the boundary into the complex-domain – see 'Managing complexity' in *KA :: Architecture as a way of thinking* (p.74). But part also, as here, would be about requirements-driven processes – as in the Japanese concept of *kanban*, or requirements-driven customised production, applied in practice by groups as diverse as Dell Computer and Toyota Motors.

For that kind of agility, methodologies like those described above become essential. Explore possibilities in your own organisation where any kind of one-off customisation – 'market-of-one' – could be applied; and then consider what type of methodology would be needed to make it work.

Resources

📖 Suzanne Robertson and James Robertson, *Mastering the Requirements Process*, Addison-Wesley, 1999, ISBN 0-201-36046-2

📖 Grady Booch, Ivar Jacobson, James Rumbaugh et al., *The Unified Software Development Process*, Addison-Wesley, 1999, ISBN 0201571692

🏛 Volere requirements methodology: www.volere.co.uk

🏛 Summary of requirements tools: www.volere.co.uk/tools.htm

🏛 DSDM: www.dsdm.org

🏛 Agile development methodologies: see www.agilealliance.org

TN :: MANAGING
SERVICES

Principles

In defining a service-oriented architecture, how will those services be managed? How does service-management intersect with your enterprise-architecture? In what ways can you leverage service-management to enhance integration across the whole architecture?

This one's fairly straightforward: a service-oriented architecture – see *KR :: The centrality of services* (p.84) – needs a systematic means to manage those services. Service-management itself should be beyond the remit of architecture, but the architecture should ensure that it matches the needs identified in the architecture.

The only complication is that of architectural scope – see *DN :: Architecture of the enterprise* (p.13) – which is dependent on architecture maturity - see *MA :: Measuring maturity* (p.123) – because this determines the range of services covered by the architecture.

At earlier architecture maturity-levels, the service-management choices will be fairly limited, for example:

- *IT-centric*: ITIL (IT Infrastructure Library), ISO 20000, AS 8015, CoBiT (Control Objectives for Information Technology)
- *industry-specific*: eTOM (enhanced Telecom Operations Map)

As maturity increases, the scope for service-management expands with the scope of the architecture. This suggests a broader range of frameworks, including:

- *generic quality-management*: TQM, Six Sigma, ISO 9000 series
- *competency models*: eSCM (eSourcing Capability Model), IT Services CMM (IT Services Capability Maturity Model), ICB (IPMA Competence Baseline)
- *project/programme management*: PMBoK, PRINCE2, MSP (Managing Successful Programmes), M_o_R (Management of Risk)

However, political problems may also increase at higher maturity-levels, as architectural integration necessarily crosses silo boundaries and encroaches on what may at times be fiercely-defended 'turf' – see *DN :: Architecture of the enterprise* (p.13) and *PA :: The politics of purpose* (p.42). Caution will be needed, particularly at key transitions in the nature and role of the architecture team – see *PL :: The architecture team* (p.34).

"For heaven's sake, why can't they follow my architecture?"

Sometimes the problem-area is architecture itself. In this instance, the team-lead was obsessed by the 'purity' of his architectural models: clarity and simplicity are important virtues, but it *is* possible to take it too far. He couldn't grasp that models describe an imaginary ideal that can never quite exist in the grubby, messy, political realities of day-to-day service-management. Instead, he blamed the rest of the world for failing to meet his idea of perfection – hence his comment above.

Something had to change – and did, fortunately for the better. The team-lead was enticed by praise to a new role elsewhere, and replaced by a leader with better political nous. He soon set up an alliance with the Programme Management Office; between them, they spun off a service-management team, who achieved full ITIL certification a short while later. A good example of how architecture can work in *practice*.

Near-real-time 'scoreboard' frameworks such Balanced Scorecard and IT Balanced Scorecard will also become more important at higher maturity levels, in order to track the state of service-management – see *MR :: Real-time scoreboards* (p.112).

Procedure

Purpose

Establish framework for management and governance of high-level service-oriented architecture.

People

Enterprise architects, senior business analysts, process architects, IT architects, programme management office.

Preparation

Standard business-analysis tools: whiteboard, meeting-space, pen and paper, time, and access to the required people.

Assessments of existing service-management methodologies and capabilities, and of the architecture scope – see *DN :: Architecture of the enterprise* (p.13).

Research on internet and other sources, for service-management methodologies and their implementations.

Process

Together with all members of the team above, select appropriate service-management frameworks and methodologies for the scope and maturity-level of the architecture and its implementation.

Identify any impacts and cross-references between the service-management frameworks and the enterprise-architecture.

Define appropriate amendments to governance processes to optimise mutual leverage between and integration of the service-management frameworks and the enterprise-architecture.

Performance (artefacts and outcomes)

Content for procedures on management and governance of services within service-oriented architecture, including alignment to selected service-management standards.

Broader applications

This perspective is *Process / Integrated* – an emphasis on mechanisms to improve integration and performance of production processes. Its direct counterpart is *Performance / Reliable*, about monitoring production and overall performance in an integrated way – see *MR :: Real-time scoreboards* (p.112).

As usual, the procedure above could apply to the whole enterprise. Many of the frameworks often described in an IT context – MSP, for example, or eTOM – do have a broader base and broader application: eTOM, for example, covers all aspects of telecoms operations, not just the specific IT subset. ISO-9000:2000 and other 'post-compliance' TQM toolsets should be relevant to any enterprise. Use the procedure above to identify appropriate frameworks for your context – and use them.

Resources

📖 IT Service Management Forum, *Frameworks for IT Management*, Van Haren, 2006, ISBN 978-90-77212-90-5 (summarises the key principles, uses and limitations of 22 frameworks, including TQM, ITIL, ISO-9001, PRINCE2, PMBoK, and Six Sigma)

🏛 ITIL: see www.itil.co.uk

🏛 itSMF: see www.itsmf.com

TR :: THE PRACTICE OF ARCHITECTURE

Principles

What will you *do* to define and implement the enterprise architecture? What methodology should you use to guide your architecture practice?

The keyword here is *practice*. This isn't about the guiding ideas, or the mindset, or whatever – for which see *DE :: Architecture on purpose* (p.21) or *KE :: Dimensions of architecture* (p.63) – but about what we *do*, and how we do it. So the three main concerns here are methodology, toolsets, and governance of compliance.

Methodology

The choice of methodology depends on the role and nature of the enterprise-architecture team – see *PL :: The architecture team* (p.34) – which in turn depends on the architecture maturity-level – see *MA :: Measuring maturity* (p.123).

As a quick summary, these are some typical methodologies for each maturity-level:

- *project-level IT architecture*: 'just enough, just in time' use of the Zachman framework
- *enterprise-wide IT architecture*: TOGAF ADM or ARIS
- *with business-architecture*: FEAF or ARIS
- *whole-of-enterprise*: 5Ps (SEMPER)

At the earlier **project-level maturity**, probably the best tactic is to use the Zachman framework together with the 'just enough, just in time' approach from DyA – Sogeti's 'Dynamic Architecture'. A warning here: Zachman is *not* sufficient on its own.

> A pleased, comforted, *certain* expression on their faces: "We're using Zachman as our methodology!"
>
> I can't count the number of times a potential client has said this to us, but it's way too often. True, Zachman's framework is comprehensive, one of the most valuable checklists around – for the IT domains, at least. But it's *only* a checklist – it doesn't *have* a methodology.

> So in the absence of anything predefined, all people can do is make one up. And the most common 'methodology' is what looks like the simplest: 'fill in the boxes'. Define every possible model, for every row and column in the framework. Just once. Then we'll have done our enterprise-architecture, won't we?
>
> Uh… no. It's slow, it's expensive, it's incredibly labour-intensive, and the only end-product is a set of all-but-meaningless models that are already out of date. They do look pretty, though…
>
> But it's then that we realise that we have to go through the process all over again, but in an imaginary world, to outline the desired 'to-be' architecture. Which is *hard*. And still meaningless, and out-of-date.
>
> And what this 'methodology' doesn't do is give the business what it wants, which is quick-wins for cost-reductions. Which, as the months and years go by with no apparent return on investment, may be why they become less and less tolerant of architecture ideas. Oops…

At this level, identify the scope of each project in terms of the Zachman framework. In most cases, it will only be two or three boxes within the Zachman grid. Then, leveraging any models that may have already been created by other projects in the same way, sketch out *only* the models that are most needed, within that subset of Zachman, and only to the edges – or preferably, if there's enough time, just over the edges – of the operational scope.

Use the models to identify quick-wins, such as easy integrations and re-use between projects. Store models in a shared repository, and document any lessons-learned, but otherwise just forget them for now. At this level, what matters most is building business trust through those quick-wins, and the architecture experience gained.

Over time, and given a diverse range of projects, this accumulates a set of models that cover the whole of the Zachman grid – but without the visible expense of 'doing Zachman', because the relevant costs have been quietly absorbed within each project.

From this base, and with the trust of the business gained, it becomes possible to attempt a more systematic *enterprise-wide* IT *architecture*. In most cases, the best methodology here is TOGAF's Architecture Design Method (ADM), though the ARIS methodology may be more useful in production-oriented environments.

Once the IT architecture has been rationalised across the enterprise, the next concern is *stronger integration with business drivers*. At present, TOGAF is still somewhat weak in that area; a better choice would be FEAF (Federal Enterprise Architecture Framework) or, again, ARIS, for a manufacturing context.

Unfortunately, none of the existing frameworks are well-suited for *whole-of-enterprise architecture*. FEAF has placeholders for 'Human Capital' and 'Other Fixed Assets' – aspects of the 'relational' and 'physical' dimensions, as in *KE :: Dimensions of architecture* (p.63) – but provides no detail beyond that; and whilst ARIS is strong in the development and production domains, it provides almost nothing for non-IT based knowledge or the 'relational' dimension in general. In practice, the methodology described in this book is almost the only available choice.

Toolsets

At early maturity-levels, it's possible to get away with modelling in Microsoft Visio and the like, supplemented as appropriate by specialist tools such as ERwin Data Modeler.

But beyond that stage, it becomes advisable, then essential, to use a purpose-built enterprise-architecture toolset. Examples include:

- Telelogic (Popkin) *System Architect* – supports TOGAF, FEAF, BPMN and other model types
- IDS Scheer *ARIS Platform* – oriented towards ARIS process methodology, but also supports some other frameworks
- BIZZDesign *BIZZDesign Architect* – supports Sogeti DyA and the ArchiMate modelling language

Toolsets are needed for cross-linking between models. Although it is technically possible to do this in Visio, it soon becomes too unwieldy to manage in practice. The purpose-built toolsets support hierarchical drill-down through nested models, and links across different model-types, and usually enforce naming conventions and other methodology requirements and constraints.

Unfortunately, none of the current toolsets as yet cover all architecture needs – especially for whole-of-enterprise architecture, as described here. Version-control is still too rudimentary in some cases. And user-interfaces still leave a lot to be desired – one toolset in particular is best described as 'user-hostile', with a dangerously fragile object-naming system and an appalling tabs-within-tabs structure for entering and editing item properties.

Some of these problems are resolved via publishing to intranet, which all of the tools do well – but in most cases only in one-way form, requiring all editing to be done by the enterprise architecture team. Two-way intranet interfaces are preferable, not least because they facilitate feedback from the 'shop floor' into the architecture – see *ME :: Closing the loop* (p.116).

Whatever the shortcomings at present, a toolset of some kind will be needed for serious enterprise-architecture. Evaluate the systems on offer, to find one that most closely matches your requirements; then design and implement workarounds as appropriate to resolve the limitations.

Governance and compliance

Architecture-models only have value if they can be used to guide real-life integration and design. Hence a significant proportion of architecture work revolves around governance and compliance, ensuring projects and systems align to the defined architectures, and seeking synergies between them wherever practicable.

Architecture governance procedures will be similar to those defined in programme-, project- or service-management frameworks such as MSP, PMBoK or ITIL – see *TN :: Managing services* (p.93). It's often best to start from within one of those frameworks, and adapt it as appropriate on the basis of experience. Some variations from the standard are likely to be needed for architecture, because the standards essentially represent 'best-practice', whereas architecture must on occasion cross over the boundary into the less-easily-defined 'probe/sense/respond' space of complex systems – see 'Management of complexity' in *KA :: Architecture as a way of thinking* (p.74).

Compliance becomes a concern from mid-level maturity onwards – in basic IT-architecture, all the work is done within individual projects, with little or no concern with external compliance. In the early stages of enterprise-wide IT architecture, there needs to be a strong if often unpopular emphasis on 'policing', with alignment reviews at project gateways – see *DR :: The architecture of the everyday* (p.17) and *PA :: The politics of purpose* (p.42) – but once the shared value of architecture is established, the emphasis should shift more to one of guidance, maintaining a 'big-picture' overview for everyone's benefit.

It's also necessary to manage 'outside of architecture' issues – applications or systems which must, for one reason or another, be non-compliant with the architecture. For example, the architecture might mandate that all mission-critical data should be maintained in enterprise-owned repositories, but a required logistics-tracking infrastructure may only be feasible in the form of an external Application Service Provider system. For each non-compliant system, document the reasons why it is permitted to be non-compliant, and identify the circumstances under which it could be brought back into alignment with the required architecture.

Procedure

Purpose

Establish and use methodology for operation, management and governance of whole-of-enterprise architecture, including the use of enterprise-architecture toolsets.

People

Selected senior managers, enterprise architects, process architects, IT architects, others as appropriate.

Preparation

Standard business-analysis tools: whiteboard, meeting-space, pen and paper, time, and access to the required people.

Research on internet and other sources, for enterprise-architecture methodologies, modelling toolsets, governance and practice.

Before you start, assess the architecture scope – see *DN :: Architecture of the enterprise* (p.13) – and maturity-level – see *MA :: Measuring maturity* (p.123).

Process

In conjunction with the team listed above, and using the architecture scope and maturity-level as a guide, select an appropriate architecture methodology. Adapt the methodology as necessary to match the operations and structure of the enterprise. Ensure that appropriate links are established with project- and programme-management, service-management, process-management and other oversight and compliance domains.

Evaluate architecture toolsets, and select an appropriate system for the present and probable future needs of the architecture. Configure the system to include intranet publication and, if practicable, intranet-based feedback into the architecture.

Use the methodology and toolset to develop models, migration-plans and the like, and to guide compliance to and integration of the architecture.

Establish a systematic review for the architecture content and the maturity and applicability of the architecture itself. In the absence of suitable procedures in the selected methodology, use a generic framework such as the TQM 'plan / do / check / act' cycle.

This process should continue indefinitely.

Performance (artefacts and outcomes)

Content for architecture models and other artefacts; procedures on operation, management and governance of enterprise architecture, including alignment to selected enterprise-architecture standards.

Broader applications

This perspective is *Process / Reliable* – a recursive emphasis on day-to-day practice, with everything that that implies in the specific work-context.

The examples and procedure above are all specific to enterprise-architecture, but the same principles would apply elsewhere:

- identifying appropriate methodologies to guide the practice – for example, workflow analysis, capability analysis, scenario development, and risk / opportunity analysis
- suitable technology to assist – the equivalents of the toolsets used in the practice of enterprise-architecture
- clear frameworks for governance and compliance, to monitor the work and any changes to procedures.

There's nothing new in this, of course: the only catch is that whilst there's often a great deal of talk about it, the real concern is to make sure that it actually *is* applied in practice.

Resources

- Zachman framework: see www.zifa.org
- DyA: see eng.dya.info/Home/
- TOGAF ADM: see www.opengroup.org/architecture/togaf8-doc/arch/toc.html
- FEAF: see www.cio.gov
- Architecture tools selection-criteria: see IFEAD, www.enterprise-architecture.info/EA_tools.htm

TL :: THE ART OF INTEGRATION

Principles

What can you use to unify every aspect of the enterprise? What theme would drive transformation, and lift performance to a whole new level?

This is one of the best ways to boost overall performance, for everyone – *if* we get it right. It's also almost independent of architecture maturity, though it works best at higher maturity-levels. The hard part is in identifying where to start: an inappropriate theme goes nowhere – though rarely does any damage – but the right one takes off in ways that are truly as spectacular.

> A routine board-level presentation, for a routine kind of project, reviewing procedures and systems at a recruitment company for compliance to new privacy legislation. About halfway through, we came to a slide about relationships with candidates, clients and others, and I described the company's role as that of a 'trusted intermediary'.
>
> Sudden silence. You could have heard a pin drop.
>
> "Can you say that again, please?" That was the managing director.
>
> "I'm saying your real role is as a trusted intermediary. It's not just one way, obtaining candidates for clients, like some kind of cannon-fodder. In many cases, your candidates *become* your clients, and they also find new clients for you. So the real issue here isn't privacy, but *trust*. If we review all the processes and so on through that lens of trust, always looking for ways to enhance that trust, what you'll have is a business model that extends itself automatically. And one that gets its income from every direction, because, for every one of your stakeholders, you act as their trusted intermediary."
>
> Again that deep, disturbing silence, finally broken once more by the managing director: "D'you reckon we could patent that?"

This is a corollary of systems-theory, particularly the concept of reflexion – see 'Systems thinking' in *KA :: Architecture as a way of thinking* (p.75). In a systems-view, every aspect of the enterprise is linked to and part of every other, in much the same that all the organs in a living body are intimately connected with and dependent on each other. So to improve overall performance, it doesn't really matter where we start, as long as we start *somewhere*.

In principle we could use any theme at all. In reality, most don't get very far: they quietly fade away to nothing. What we're after is something *self-propagating* – the 'snowball effect' from that other systems-principle of resonance. To do this, the theme must:

- be *universal* – applies to every aspect of the enterprise
- be *emotive* in some way
- be *directly applicable* in everyday, personal work
- be applicable *iteratively*, permitting continuous improvement
- be *measurable*, such that improvements can be tracked

Probably the best example is a focus on quality. W Edwards Deming used it in a number of variations – *kaizen*, *kanban* and so on – to transform Japanese industry. Jack Welch used it to create Six Sigma at General Electric. It engages everyone; it's real, measurable, tangible; it works. But it isn't the only option: others I've used include:

- client trust in privacy – as in the story above
- client trust in delivery – reliability of logistics
- corrective action – process improvement
- 'single source of truth' – data quality and data management
- waste-reduction – time, money, materials, other resources

What works best is something that matches the needs and mood of the enterprise. Jack Welch selected several such themes in his tenure at General Electric, but only ever *one* theme at a time, and each for only three to five years. Sometimes a theme presents itself as 'the obvious thing to do'; for others, it can be helpful to conduct some kind of narrative-inquiry such as Open Space – see *PE :: What's the story?* (p.57) – to elicit an appropriate theme from within the collective tacit knowledge of the enterprise.

Another key advantage of this type of integration strategy is that it tends to pull the power-dynamics toward the functional end of the spectrum – see *PR :: A problem of power* (p.47). Part of this is from the natural enthusiasm of the 'local champions' who take on the strategy as their own – see *PA :: The politics of purpose* (p.42). But it's also because the theme engages people personally and emotively in new ways of looking at their work, and makes the work inherently feel more worthwhile – the same driver for con-structive change as in *DL :: Architecture is a feeling* (p.30).

Procedure

Purpose

Identify and establish frameworks to use one or more unifying 'themes' for whole-of-organisation integration.

People

Selected senior managers, strategists, enterprise architects, change management specialists, others as appropriate (especially any local 'champions' for a selected unifying theme).

Preparation

Standard business-analysis tools: whiteboard, meeting-space, pen and paper, time, and access to the required people.

If appropriate, conduct narrative-enquiry – see *PE :: What's the story?* (p.57) – to elicit candidate themes.

Process

Together with all members of the team above, brainstorm and review potential themes for whole-of-organisation integration.

Verify each candidate against the checklist above: universal, emotive, personal, applicable, iterative and measurable. Identify metrics to monitor improved performance in an overt, easily-understandable form – see *MR :: Real-time scoreboards* (p.112).

With the assistance of selected local 'champions', pilot-test potential changes to procedures and feedback – see *ME :: Closing the loop* (p.116) – using the complexity principle of 'probe / sense / respond' – see 'Managing complexity' in *KA :: Architecture as a way of thinking* (p.74) – and providing appropriate support for knowledge-sharing – see *PE :: What's the story?* (p.57) and *KL :: A question of responsibility* (p.80).

If a selected theme seems to self-propagate appropriately, roll out into broader usage, ideally to the scale of the entire enterprise.

Monitor and repeat as required.

Performance (artefacts and outcomes)

Strategy-level and tactics-level plans for roll-out of selected unifying theme, including content for change-management, risk/opportunity management and governance.

Broader applications

This perspective is *Process / Elegant* – an emphasis on the use of emotive 'themes' and other tactics to drive process-improvement. Its direct counterpart is *People / Reliable*, about tactics to make the actions of and interactions between people easier and more productive – see *PR :: A problem of power* (p.47).

The description and procedure are not only for any aspect of the enterprise, but ideally should always apply to the *whole* enterprise. That's how it works best, not only because it improves integration anyway, but because by engaging *everyone* in the emerging conversation, the maximum possible range of ideas and experiences can be brought to bear on any issue or problem. Other useful 'themes' here can include 'post-compliance' TQM such as such as quality-circles; an emphasis on occupational health and safety, environment; ergonomics, and personalisation, both within the organisation – such as integrated performance-support systems – and outside – such as 'market of one' customisation.

The guiding principle for choice of 'theme' is as described above: "what works best is something that matches the needs and mood of the enterprise at the time". It's essential, then, to listen out for hints and signals about the changing nature of the enterprise, to catch the right moment to inject an appropriate 'theme'. As above, large-group interventions such as Open Space are probably the most valuable tactics to use here; but in the absence of those, or a lack of maturity to enable such tactics to be safely used, monitor the mood via some other means such as the SEMPER whole-of-context diagnostic – see *ML :: People and performance* (p.119) – and use the results to identify an appropriate intervention.

Resources

📖 Jack Welch at GE: see Robert Slater, *Jack Welch & The G.E. Way: Management Insights and Leadership Secrets of the Legendary CEO*, McGraw-Hill, 1998, ISBN 0070581045

📖 Peter M Sengé et al., *The Fifth Discipline Fieldbook: Strategies and tools for building a learning organization*, Currency (1994), ISBN-13 978-0385472562.

🏛 Open Space: www.openspaceworld.org

🏛 TQM: see www.managementhelp.org/quality/tqm/tqm.htm

TA :: WHAT'S THE SCORE?

Principles

How can you ensure that each strategy supports every aspect of the enterprise?

This is another straightforward section that can be applied at any maturity-level. What we need here is some means to assess the probable impact of a strategy or tactic, not only on the immediate area of interest, but on the *whole* enterprise.

The standard tool for this is SWOT – the old checklist of Strengths, Weaknesses, Opportunities, Threats. It does work well for quick, simple assessments; but it's a bit *too* quick, *too* simple, too 'us and them', for the depth and complexity of many of the issues we deal with in enterprise-architecture. Some of the changes we'd need:

- *make the language more real* – not 'weaknesses' or 'threats'
- *adapt for use in broader, more complex contexts* – in multi-organisation enterprises, partnerships and value-webs, boundaries between 'inside' and 'outside' are often blurred
- *adapt for a more holistic view* – assess impact on overall effectiveness: how does each asset or concern interact with others?
- *enhance the methodology* – iterative review with qualitative and quantitative scores, or 'before and after' comparisons

And we need it to work at every level, every scale – see *DR :: The architecture of the everyday* (p.17).

We can do this by reworking SWOT as 'SCORE'.

- We look at what we already have – our existing **S**trengths.
- We look at what we know we need, or need to address – our **C**hallenges.
- We look *to* the outside world for our **O**ptions and opportunities.
- We also look at the probable **R**esponses *from* the outside world to the chosen strategy.
- We explore the probable impacts of the strategy on overall **E**ffectiveness.

Where this differs from SWOT is that we do this *iteratively*, comparing each dimension against the others.

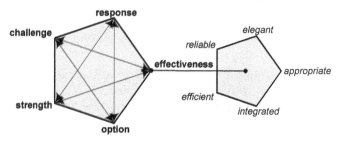

SCORE methodology

This gives us an iterative methodology that we can summarise in the diagram above – and is also similar to the 5Ps framework we're using here for enterprise-architecture as a whole.

First, we select a suitable issue to work with. Although we'd generally use a current strategy for this, in practice almost anything will do, because ultimately everything is connected to everything else - see *TL :: The art of integration* (p.102).

Once we've selected the issue, we can start the checklist anywhere, though it's usual to start with Strengths, or Options. We then work our way through all the SCORE dimensions, repeating and iterating in any order, and using the viewpoint of each dimension as a perspective on each of the other dimensions.

For everything we identify, we assess impact on *overall* effectiveness, with the checklist of efficient, reliable, elegant, appropriate, integrated – see *KN :: An emphasis on effectiveness* (p.69).

We also keep an eye open for anything that can be measured, whether as a numeric value or qualitatively – for example, a new capability that didn't exist at the time of a previous SCORE assessment. The reason is that it's much easier to manage things that can be measured.

Strengths, services, support

The questions for the Strengths dimension are much the same as for SWOT, except we need to look both inside *and outside* the organisation for *shared* strengths and support:

- *Strengths* – What would we regard as our strengths in this?
- *Services* – What services and capabilities do we have? What services can we call on from others?

- *Support* – What support-resources do we have available to us? What support do we have from others?

The work of projects is carried out through services and capabilities, so these questions also help us to identify the components for a service-oriented architecture for the enterprise – see *KR :: The centrality of services* (p.84).

The subsidiary questions about support here are essential. Without explicit support from senior management, the project can only be run as a concealed 'skunk-works', which would be a political risk – see *PA :: The politics of purpose* (p.42) – and would mean a lot more work overall – see *PR :: A problem of power* (p.47).

This dimension should provide us with an inventory of what we have available to respond to opportunities and to support the change-roadmap, and a list of probable partners in the project.

Challenges, capabilities needed

The questions for the Challenges dimension are again similar to SWOT. But we avoid SWOT's pejorative term 'weakness' here, instead thinking more of 'challenge' in the scientific sense: "a condition of the environment that regulates growth", or "an opportunity to improve". This allows us to concentrate more on gap-analysis, on identifying what we would need to achieve the key success criteria for the project.

- *Challenges* – What are the issues we need to address? within the organisation? in relationships with partners, suppliers, other stakeholders?
- *Capabilities needed* – What new capabilities and services would we need? What skills would be required? What would be needed to develop these skills and services?

This gives us a list of needed capabilities – the content for the change-roadmap – and also identifies the *internal* project-risks.

Options, opportunities and risks

Opportunities give rise to options, which in turn provide the basis for a roadmap for change.

As with SWOT, we should be looking outward here, at the 'outside' world of potential customers, partners, providers and the like. But unlike SWOT, we assess opportunities and risks *together*, because each is the flipside of the other. Opportunities bring concomitant risks; and risks – SWOT's 'threats' – always present us with opportunities.

- *Opportunities* – What opportunities present themselves? What risks arise from and with those opportunities? What opportunities arise from apparent risks?
- *Options* – What are our options in relation to those opportunities and risks? How can we act on the options? How should we prioritise the options and actions?

This identifies the reasons or requirements for the change, and the priorities for those requirements in the change-roadmap – see *TE :: Requirements for agility* (p.89). It should also indicate the *external* project-risks arising from those opportunities.

What we're looking at, and looking *for*, are the drivers for business change: opportunities and risks, and options to respond to each.

Responses, regulations, returns, rewards

Where 'Opportunities' is about how we respond to the outside world, the 'Responses' questions are more about how the outside world impinges on us. For example, even a brief focus on regulation and legislation helps to expand our awareness of longer-term impacts: legislation may move at a much slower pace than business cycles, but its impacts cannot be avoided forever.

- *Responses* – What responses would we expect from customers? from competitors? from providers? from partners? from other stakeholders?
- *Regulations* – What regulations might arise in response to the strategy? What would be the impacts of new or upcoming legislation?
- *Returns and rewards* – What is the business value of each opportunity and risk?

We also need to explore responses to what *doesn't* happen as a result of the strategy, such as opportunity-costs and cost-savings – for example, see 'Connections' in *PE :: What's the story?* (p.57)

If possible, we need to describe these expected responses in *measurable* terms, identifying the overall returns or rewards. In other words, this dimension identifies the business-case – if any – for the strategy, and further external risks impinging *indirectly* on the opportunities.

Effectiveness

The Effectiveness questions are the key difference from conventional SWOT analysis – see *KN :: An emphasis on effectiveness* (p.69).

The aim is to resolve a classic business dilemma: how to ensure that improvements in one area do not cause greater inefficiencies elsewhere – a common result of traditional analysis techniques.

- *Efficient* – Does the strategy optimise use of resources, minimise wastage of resources?
- *Reliable* – Is the result of the strategy predictable, consistent, self-correcting?
- *Elegant* – Does the strategy support simplicity, clarity, consistency, self-adaptation for human factors?
- *Appropriate* – Does the strategy optimise support for business purpose?
- *Integrated* – Does the strategy create, support and optimise synergy across all systems?

This dimension should identify how well the 'as-is' and 'to-be' systems fit in with everything else.

Outcomes

At the end of the SCORE assessment, these are the documents we would expect to have, to guide subsequent change.

- *Strengths* – capabilities/services inventory, support/partner-map
- *Challenges* – prioritised roadmap for change, risks/issues register
- *Options* – strategy scenarios, opportunity/risk trade-off register
- *Responses* – business case, risk-management scenarios
- *Effectiveness* – project impact/integration assessments

The end-product of a SCORE assessment is a clear roadmap for business change.

Procedure

Purpose

Establish framework for strategic and architectural assessment of cross-functional effectiveness.

People

Enterprise architects, strategists, process architects, IT architects, lead trainers, others as appropriate (mainly operations specialists).

Preparation

Standard business-analysis tools: whiteboard, meeting-space, pen and paper, time, and access to the required people.

Process

Select a strategic issue to assess.

In conjunction with others as appropriate, use the SCORE methodology outlined above to assess the impact and options for the strategy, and to compare against any previous assessments of the same or a similar strategy.

Document the results as indicated under 'Outcomes' above.

Optionally, in conjunction with lead-trainers, develop training-materials to roll out the use of the SCORE methodology to wider use within the enterprise.

Performance (artefacts and outcomes)

Strategic assessments; content for training materials in strategic assessment of cross-functional effectiveness.

Broader applications

This perspective is *Process / Appropriate* – an emphasis on effectiveness and relevance of day-to-day tasks. Its counterpart is *Purpose / Reliable*, about the 'physicalness' and realisation of business purpose – see DR :: *The architecture of the everyday* (p.17).

The SCORE methodology can be applied to strategic reviews in every context of the enterprise: if you think of it as 'SWOT on effectiveness', its usage should become immediately clear. Its aim is to ensure that every task is done 'on purpose', which is why clarity on enterprise purpose – see DE :: *Architecture on purpose* (p.21) – should be a first concern here.

Resources

✸ SCORE: see www.tetradian.com/score

MR :: REAL-TIME SCOREBOARDS

Principles

In what ways can the architecture guide the monitoring of real-time performance? How do you ensure that the most relevant, meaningful and accurate metrics are used? How do these metrics reflect the performance of the *whole* of the enterprise?

This is primarily the domain of broad-scope performance monitoring frameworks such as 'Balanced Scorecard' and its IT-centric variant 'IT Balanced Scorecard'. It's not really the role of architects to specify the metrics to be used here, though at higher maturity-levels, as cross-enterprise generalists, the team should certainly be involved. But ensuring that the systems do properly support the use of those metrics is a valid task for enterprise-architecture.

> Cross-enterprise scorecards can be tricky things at best, because to work well they need a generalist's eye for the whole. Watching a bunch of bean-counters try to define a Balanced Scorecard can often seem a sad experience, because the whole point is that it disrupts the delusion that money is the sole measure of the world.
>
> But my favourite example of a Balanced Scorecard disaster-area was at an engineering research establishment. They were struggling to select appropriate criteria for inclusion in the organisation-wide scorecard: how exactly could they be certain that a putative 'key performance indicator' really *was* 'key'? So, being good scientists, they set up a sub-committee to create a mathematical formula to derive a numeric value for 'key-ness'. Which, since the criteria in question were all about human factors, and blurry shades of grey, seemed a somewhat extreme case of missing the point…

The basic Balanced Scorecard framework, as described by Kaplan and Norton, has four distinct perspectives:

- *financial perspective* – "how do we look to shareholders?"
- *customer perspective* – "how do customers see us?"
- *internal business-process perspective* – "what must we excel at?"
- *learning and growth perspective* – "how can we continue to improve and create value?"

Interestingly, it's arguable whether 'financial perspective' has a useful purpose in Balanced Scorecard, as shareholder-value has long been understood to be a poor indicator of future performance – "the Bermuda Triangle of strategy", as Michael Porter put it. It's also a complex derivative outcome, a rearward-looking 'lag-indicator' rather than a forward-looking 'lead indicator' like the other three – see *ML :: People and performance* (p.119). From a dimensions viewpoint – see *KE :: Dimensions of architecture* (p.63) – the 'financial perspective' would be more usefully replaced by a 'purpose perspective' – see *DE :: Architecture on purpose* (p.21).

But given scorecard-metrics selected by enterprise performance-specialists, the main architectural concerns would be:

- *single point of truth* – raw-data for metrics to be derived from verified master-sources such as a 'database of record' (DBoR)
- *audit trail of derivation* – all processes and business-rules used to transform raw-data to scorecard-metrics are identified and monitored

The latter would include identifying the data-owners, process-owners, business-rule owners and the like – see *KL :: A question of responsibility* (p.80) and, in conjunction with the programme management and others, monitoring governance of data and its transforms – see 'Governance and compliance' in *TR :: The practice of architecture* (p.99). The original Balanced Scorecard specification indicates that metrics should also be linked to the missions and objectives of the respective 'purpose audit-trail' – see *DE :: Architecture on purpose* (p.21).

Procedure

Purpose

Establish framework and metrics to track whole-of-organisation integration and cross-functional performance in real-time.

People

Enterprise architects, process architects, IT architects, performance specialists.

Preparation

Standard business-analysis tools: whiteboard, meeting-space, pen and paper, time, and access to the required people.

Process

In conjunction with other architects, assist the performance-specialists in identifying appropriate metrics and the respective data-sources and transforms.

Identify and specify requirements for any amendments to systems to support 'single source of truth' for each required data-source.

Model and verify the 'audit-trail of derivation' for each metric, including governance of each step in the trail of derivations and transforms.

Performance (artefacts and outcomes)

List of required metrics, including identification of required data-sources, data-capture processes and business-rules for data-transform.

Broader applications

This perspective is *Performance / Reliable* – an emphasis on monitoring production and overall performance in an integrated way. Its direct counterpart is *Process / Integrated*, about mechanisms to improve the integration and overall performance of production processes – see *TN :: Managing services* (p.93).

The same general principles as above apply throughout the enterprise: Balanced Scorecard is a good start for most contexts, though it's not the only choice. The key concern is to find *lead*-indicators which point toward future performance: most of the usual metrics are *lag*-indicators, pointing only to the past, which are of little use here. The one metric that in general should *not* be used for this purpose is financial performance: it's valid in its own way, of course, but as a complex outcome with no direct causal linkage to action, it tells us nothing about what to *do* to create improvements in real-time.

One of the minor dangers in this perspective is that it's easy to look only at IT for suitable metrics. It's important to also include human-centred information, so as to garner appropriate human-centred metrics. Online tools such as intranets, extranets, wikis, weblogs and social-network maps can be useful here; likewise

active support for dialogue and narrative-knowledge – see *PE ::
What's the story?* (p.57) – and, if circumstances permit, large-group
interventions such as Future Search and Open Space – see *ML ::
People and performance* (p.119)..

Resources

📖 Robert Kaplan & David Norton, *The Balanced Scorecard:
Translating Strategy into Action*, Harvard Business School Press,
1996, ISBN 0875846513

🏯 Balanced Scorecard: www.balancedscorecard.org

🏯 IT Balanced Scorecard: see IT Governance Institute, www.itgi.org

ME :: CLOSING THE LOOP

Principles

How do you validate the architecture? What processes would you use to obtain and incorporate feedback from the architecture's stakeholders? How can you use the architecture itself to drive a process of continuous learning and growth?

What this is really about is enhancing the effectiveness of the architecture – see *KN :: An emphasis on effectiveness* (p.69). To do this, we need not merely to publish what we've done and developed, but make it accessible in a way that engages everyone in developing it further, and in making it their own.

This is the means by which the architecture becomes *dynamic*, both reflecting and driving the ever-changing needs of the enterprise.

It's here, unfortunately, that we're badly let down by the existing toolsets for enterprise-architecture.

Without exception, it seems, their 'user-interfaces' are almost too awkward to use. Either there's no means to enforce the required rigour, or we're forced to struggle with a cumbersome monstrosity that only a programmer could love. Letting ordinary users loose on these tools is a recipe for full-on frustration all round – and a mess that can take months to clean up, as I know from painful experience...

Almost all the tools *do* have web-publishing tools, with drill-down and crosslinking and so on. But most only work one way – there's no direct means to get comments and feedback back *into* the architecture. Which means frustrated clients who feel they're being talked *at* rather than talked *with*. Which means we don't get the engagement we need. Which becomes a *big* problem if we're not careful.

Often the only way to guarantee getting the feedback we need is to go out and ask for it, in person. Which is labour-intensive, expensive in time, and all the rest.

Frustrating, to say the least.

Annoyingly, existing methodologies don't seem to be strong on this obvious need. Phase H, 'Architecture Change Management', in the TOGAF Architectural Design Method does cover this issue to some extent, but doesn't tell us anything about what to *do* here.

In effect, what we need is similar to narrative inquiry – see *PE :: What's the story?* (p.57). In my own work, the method I use most for this is one of the simplest: the US Army's 'After Action Review' (AAR). An AAR consists of just four questions:

- What was supposed to happen?
- What actually happened?
- What caused the difference?
- What could we learn from this?

It doesn't need sophisticated equipment: it can be done anywhere, with anyone, with answers scribbled on the back of envelope if need be. Spend perhaps a quarter of the time on the first two questions; a quarter of the time on the third; and the remainder on the last – which we could also rephrase as "What could we do differently next time?"

There's just one rule for an AAR, which the Army describes as "pin your stripes to the door". It doesn't matter who we are, what supposed 'rank' we might have: we each have our own part to play, our own responsibility – see *KL :: A question of responsibility* (p.80) – and the aim of the review is to help *everyone* improve.

Having gathered the feedback, we need governance procedures to guide what aspects of the feedback should be incorporated into the revision of the architecture. But however we do it, it's essential that people *see* their feedback is valued, driving a 'virtuous spiral' of engagement – see *PA :: The politics of purpose* (p.42).

Procedure

Purpose

Establish framework for feedback into enterprise-architecture.

People

Enterprise architects, process-architects, IT architects, knowledge managers, change-managers, programme management office, others as appropriate (particularly project-managers and local 'champions').

Preparation

Standard business-analysis tools: whiteboard, meeting-space, pen and paper, time, and access to the required people.

Research on internet and elsewhere for strategies and tactics to garner feedback into the architecture.

Process

In conjunction with the full range of architecture stakeholders, assess methods to capture and incorporate feedback into the architecture. Include processes for governance of such amendments to architectural models and other artefacts.

From this review, select appropriate procedures, and pilot-test them in practice with local 'champions'.

Amend the procedures on the basis of the pilot-tests, and roll out the amended feedback procedures to the wider community.

Performance (artefacts and outcomes)

Content for feedback procedures and procedures for governance of enterprise-architecture and its amendment.

Broader applications

This perspective is *Performance / Efficient* – an emphasis on the ways in which shared knowledge can be used to pull the enterprise together. Its direct counterpart is *Preparation / Integrated*, about using an awareness of the whole to drive process improvement – see *KN :: An emphasis on effectiveness* (p.69).

We should be able to use the same principles, and most of the same practices, to improve performance across the whole enterprise. Collison and Parcell's book *Learning To Fly* gives good, practical examples of 'learning before doing', 'learning whilst doing' and 'learning after doing' – the After Action Review being one technique for the latter. Benchmarking, real-time 'dashboards' and integration frameworks can also help here. But there are plenty of other useful techniques to elicit, collate and act on feedback: find them and use them.

Resources

📖 After Action Review: see Chris Collison and Geoff Parcell, *Learning To Fly: practical lessons from one of the world's leading knowledge companies*, Capstone, 2001; ISBN-13 978-184112509-1

🕸 TOGAF ADM: see www.opengroup.org/architecture/togaf8-doc/arch/toc.html

ML :: PEOPLE AND PERFORMANCE

Principles

What is the organisation's ability to do work? How would you measure and monitor this?

Financial figures and the like are useful, of course, but they're rearward-looking 'lag-indicators' that tell us where we've been – whereas what we need are 'lead-indicators' that tell us whether we're on track to where we want to go. So what we're looking for here are metrics that point to *future* performance – especially about people and the collective 'ability to do work'.

> Guess I should know better, but I'm still amazed at how often I see a so-called strategy that amounts to "last year's figures plus ten percent".
>
> It's not a strategy. It's a target – an arbitrary target plucked out of nowhere. It's not even linked to the enterprise's vision. And it tells us nothing – *nothing* – about how to get to that target. No wonder that kind of 'strategy' so rarely works well...
>
> Financial metrics are a complex outcome of a complex world in which nothing can ever truly be controlled. They indicate only what happened in the past, with no clear causal linkage to the future at all. Surely even the most rudimentary common-sense would suggest it's not wise to try to steer a large, complex enterprise solely on the basis of what's visible in the rear-view mirror? But apparently not, because we still see supposedly-bright business-people doing it every day. Hence the all-too-frequent occurrence of what's commonly called a 'crash'. Ouch...

The 'people-stuff' is important because of what I've once seen described bitterly as 'presenteeism': people may be present in body, but that'll be about it if we don't properly address the power-issues and other emotive issues – see, for example, *PA :: The politics of purpose* (p.42), *DL :: Architecture is a feeling* (p.30) or *PE :: What's the story?* (p.57). But if we *do* address those issues appropriately, the amount of 'ability to do work' is enormous: dismay and distrust can be infectious, but so are enthusiasm and commitment when conditions are right. So the states of the various people-issues are perhaps the most powerful and reliable lead-indicators of future performance that we have.

The simplest metric of all is a straightforward staff-survey: properly used and properly understood, even that will probably tell you more than all the financial forecasts put together. The consultancy firm Human Synergistics took this a strong step forward with its LSI metric, or Life Styles Inventory, which provides a kind of compass of decision-making styles within the organisation, and the impacts that these will have on productivity and performance. And there are a fair few others around, such as the diagnostic in Richard Barrett's 'Liberating The Corporate Soul' framework, originally developed for the World Bank.

Another is the SEMPER diagnostic and intervention-design tool, which arose from the work I've done with large organisations over the past few decades. Rather than focusing direct on the people, as in the LSI diagnostic or Richard Barrett's work, it uses people's views of the overall context as an indirect – and hence politically safer – means to identify 'ability to do work'. In effect, the views are a kind of *reflexion*, seeing the whole reflected in even the smallest part – see 'Systems thinking' in *KA :: Architecture as a way of thinking* (p.75). As described further on the Tetradian website, the 'ability to do work' from each perspective is assessed in terms of the same power-model we're using here – see *PR :: A problem of power* (p. 47); the Australian consultant Holly Dinh provided the key concept of assessment by 'word-pictures' or emotive phrases than an arbitrary numeric scale. The full version of SEMPER uses the complete set of dimensions and link-themes that make up the structure of the enterprise – see *KE :: Dimensions of architecture* (p.63) – whilst the simpler SEMPER-5 has the same base framework as in this book.

Whatever tool is used, the metric has little meaning on its own. Its purpose is to guide what to do next, to enhance the organisation's ability to do work, to resolve skills-gaps and so on. SEMPER-5, for example, is mapped to a comprehensive set of intervention strategies and tactics which would be used to address the respective issues. Large-group interventions such as Open Space and Future Search are probably the most powerful of all tools, but can only be used safely when the metric indicates an absence of any serious power-problems in the respective areas of the enterprise. Which is why this type of metric is essential for the development of organisational integration.

Procedure

Purpose

Establish framework for monitoring cross-functional 'ability to do work'.

People

Enterprise architects, HR specialists, performance specialists.

Preparation

Standard business-analysis tools: whiteboard, meeting-space, pen and paper, time, and access to the required people.

Research on internet and elsewhere for lead-indicator metrics on human performance and methods to elicit them.

Process

In conjunction with HR specialists and performance specialists, review the available methods to derive metrics for pointers to future human performance.

Select one or more suitable methods. Where appropriate, adapt the metrics to suit the specific needs of the enterprise.

Specify requirements to incorporate the selected metrics into regular reporting, such as a Balanced Scorecard – see *MR :: Real-time scoreboards* (p.112). Pass these requirements to the Programme Management Office, or equivalent, for implementation.

Performance (artefacts and outcomes)

List of required metrics, including identification of required data-sources, data-capture processes and business-rules for data-transform.

Broader applications

This perspective is *Performance / Elegant* – an emphasis on the impact of people and people-issues on overall performance. Its counterpart is *People / Integrated*, about how these issues help to pull the enterprise together into an integrated whole – see *PN :: The role of the generalist* (p.52).

The principles and procedure above are generic to the whole enterprise, of course. But whilst I've emphasised 'people-metrics' here, the people-issues can be often be broader than that: concerns such as ergonomics and workflow, for example, can have a real impact on overall performance. Cynefin narrative-enquiry – see *PE :: What's the story?* (p.57) – and social sense-making – see 'Managing complexity' in *KA :: Architecture as a way of thinking* (p.74) – can also be useful techniques to identify potential problems before they turn critical; likewise ensuring equity and diversity policy are put into visible practice.

There would also be risk-management concerns about overall performance being too dependent on individual skills in specific processes. One example that comes to mind was a café way back in my student days: they managed a high throughput because of one person who was extraordinarily fast at serving up. When he left, service slowed to a crawl; would-be customers walked out, and the café became so unprofitable it went out of business.

There's another corollary here to the Peter Principle – "people are promoted to their level of incompetence" – that traps competent people in low-level, denigrated roles; when they finally give up in disgust, the system can often grind to a halt. It's important to watch out for these kinds of subtle cross-dependencies: they can cripple overall performance, without apparent warning, if the performance-tracking systems fail to pick them up in time.

Resources

- Large group interventions: see Martin Leith, www.largegroupinterventions.com/documents/leiths_guide_to_lgis.pdf
- Human Synergistics: www.human-synergistics.com.au/content/products/diagnostics/lsi.asp
- Richard Barrett: www.valuescentre.org
- SEMPER diagnostic: www.tetradian.com/semper
- Cynefin narrative-enquiry and sense-making: see Cognitive Edge at www.cognitive-edge.com

MA :: MEASURING MATURITY

Principles

What is the current maturity of your enterprise-architecture? What is its most appropriate scope? And what next steps do you need to take to extend that maturity and scope?

Maturity-metrics do provide useful indicators as to the probable value of the architecture to the enterprise – see *MN :: Monitoring integration* (p.126). But their real purpose is much simpler, namely to guide what to develop next:

- changes to the team – see *PL :: The architecture team* (p.34)
- changes to scope – see *DN :: Architecture of the enterprise* (p.13)
- changes to architecture practice – see *TR :: The practice of architecture* (p.96)
- changes to the guiding ideas and perspectives – see *KA :: Architecture as a way of thinking* (p.73), *KE :: Dimensions of architecture* (p.63) and *DL :: Architecture is a feeling* (p.30)

As with development in any living organism, each improvement in maturity provides stepping-stones to the next. But there's a definite pattern to these stepping-stones: although we can often vary the sequence in which we tackle them, few can be skipped entirely without causing greater problems later on. For example, we can't link to business-drivers until we *have* sorted out the basic technical architecture; we can't support agility until we have a proper version-controlled requirements repository in place. A maturity-model provides a map of where we are amongst those stepping-stones, and which ones to choose next.

> One of the most comprehensive models for early- to mid-level architecture-maturity is M E van Steenbergen's *DyA Architecture Maturity Matrix*. It's available free from Sogeti, part of the CapGemini consultancy, and provided in the form of an Excel workbook and matching descriptive document.
>
> It's IT-centric, and doesn't cover all of the more complex late-maturity whole-of-enterprise-architecture. But for the earlier stages, it's more than sufficient: over 130 questions, more than 50 steps, in 18 distinct

streams such as 'Defining architecture', 'Involvement of business' and 'Coordination of activities', and cross-mapped to 13 levels of maturity. Some of her sequences can seem a little odd in places, and may need tweaking to match the enterprise needs – but if nothing else, it's a great way to get the architecture-dialogue going. Recommended.

The fine detail in a maturity-model is useful to indicate the small steps need to underpin continuous improvement. However, there are four distinct levels that are quantum jumps, requiring radical changes to the role and nature of the team, the reporting relationships and the architectural mindset and practice:

- *project-level IT-architecture* – exists only as part of project brief, minimal coordination between projects
- *enterprise-wide IT architecture* – strong centralised coordination across IT domains (primarily applications and infrastructure)
- *enterprise IT-architecture with business-architecture* – splits into layer-specific sub-teams (data, applications, technology), small coordinating team links IT to business strategy
- *whole-of-enterprise architecture* – coordinating team moves out of IT, creates links across all IT and non-IT domains

At the least, the maturity-model used needs to identify the overall maturity in these terms above.

Procedure

Purpose

Establish frameworks and metrics to monitor performance and maturity of enterprise-architecture.

People

Enterprise architects, knowledge managers, performance specialists.

Preparation

Standard business-analysis tools: whiteboard, meeting-space, pen and paper, time, and access to the required people.

Research on internet and other sources, for methods, techniques and frameworks for assessing enterprise-architecture maturity.

Before you start, assess the architecture scope – see *DN :: Architecture of the enterprise* (p.13).

Process

Together with knowledge managers and performance specialists, review the available tools to assess architectural maturity.

Select a suitable tool. Where appropriate, adapt its metrics to suit the specific needs of the enterprise.

If previous assessments have been undertaken, map and migrate the metrics and values as necessary to those of the selected tool.

Using the tool, conduct an assessment of architecture maturity. In conjunction with the tool's framework, use the results of the assessment to identify any appropriate changes to the architecture team, scope, or practice.

Performance (artefacts and outcomes)

List of required metrics, including identification of required data-sources, data-capture processes and business-rules for data-transform; assessments of architecture maturity; recommendations for changes to architecture team, scope, practice, etcetera.

Broader applications

This perspective is *Performance / Appropriate* – an emphasis on measuring integration or 'togetherness' of the enterprise. Its direct counterpart is *Purpose / Integrated*, about purpose providing a focus to align the enterprise with itself, and also identifying that 'togetherness' – see DN :: *Architecture of the enterprise* (p.13).

Maturity-metrics are amongst the most useful tools here. Those listed above are specific to enterprise-architecture, but each industry and domain has its own: eSCM, IT Services CMM and ICB, for example, are three IT-industry examples listed in *TN :: Managing services* (p.93). It's also useful to map these metrics into real-time 'dashboards' that can be used to support values / performance reviews. The essential point is that these are not metrics for their own sake: their purpose is to provide guidance, indicating appropriate steps for further development.

Resources

- Sogeti maturity matrix: see
  eng.dya.info/Home/services/architecture_maturity_model.zip
- TOGAF maturity model: see www.opengroup.org/architecture/togaf8-doc/arch/toc.html

MN :: MONITORING INTEGRATION

Principles

How can you demonstrate the value of enterprise-architecture? What is the architecture worth to the enterprise as a whole?

This one's always going to be hard. No surprises in that, because architecture isn't a production environment – it supports production, but doesn't produce anything itself – so will always be seen first as a cost. As with risk-management, most of the value gained is in terms of what *didn't* happen – which is much harder to prove and to quantify *because* it didn't happen.

> Sometimes even accounting systems can conspire against us in this...
>
> At one of our clients, a large multi-national, only the largest systems were listed as line-items – perhaps a dozen of them, averaging half a billion dollars each. All the other systems – hundreds of them, with a combined value of several billion dollars – were lumped together under a single line-item labelled 'Other'. And there was no way to separate out a specific value for any one of these smaller systems.
>
> For this project, the business-case was based on the cost-savings from decommissioning duplicate systems. But there was no way we could prove it. The decommissioning costs showed up all right – but not the savings, because they vanished into that all-consuming 'Other'.
>
> Demonstrable cost less no demonstrable savings equals no business case. So even though it was obvious that the savings were real, and significant, we never did get the go-ahead to finish the project.
>
> Crazy.

The remainder of the value gained comes from integration, from synergies across systems, services and organisational silos; and also, as with knowledge-management, from making it possible for the right things to happen.

As follows, the value-proposition shifts with the maturity-level – see *MA :: Measuring maturity* (p.123).

Project-level IT-architecture

The main visible value here comes from decommissioning, usually of single medium-sized legacy systems. Projects should be selected to provide visible 'quick wins'. Establish the direct current and future cost of operating the existing system, such as licence costs, maintenance, training etcetera. Project-costs should be low enough to make the business-case visible and viable.

Some value will also be obtained from work on standardisation, simplification, and coordination between projects, but this is unlikely to be quantifiable in the terms required for a business-case.

Enterprise-wide IT architecture

The key targets at this level are the myriad of small reporting systems and single-function custom-built applications – perhaps thousands of them, in a large organisation – which drive critical day-to-day production but have innumerable fragile links with other systems. Although cutting maintenance costs – and, often, dangerous dependencies on individuals – has demonstrable financial returns, the real *business* value will come from reducing the 'hassle': catch-phrases such as "cutting through the spaghetti" and "single source of truth" will often be useful here.

> Sometimes avoidance of embarrassment at high levels can become a most immediate business driver.
>
> In one spectacular example, the Government presented a shining set of figures for a government department; yet the Opposition found a different set of figures, supposedly from the same source, but painting a far less rosy picture. Would the Minister please explain this difference, they said? Was the Minister misleading the public, perhaps? Angry phone calls from the Minister to the department heads; demands for immediate explanation; red faces all round...
>
> Turned out that everyone was right – sort of. Both sets of figures did come from the same source – sort of – but had gone through different transforms and business-rules, without a controlled audit-trail, ending up in different reporting-systems but purporting to be the same. Oops.
>
> We'd previously struggled to get the go-ahead for abstract-projects such as 'single source of truth' and 'database of record'. But for a while there, these suddenly seemed to gain a very high value – not far off a no-questions-asked business-case, in fact. Can't think why...

At this level, important work will also be done on establishing the ground-base for data-standards, code re-use, the first stages of a service-oriented architecture and such. Don't expect anyone outside IT to understand the value of this, though.

Enterprise IT-architecture with business-architecture

Although the focus is still primarily on IT, much of the IT-specific work is split off at this stage. Most of the value of this *enterprise-*

level architecture is as an interface between the business proper, the project teams, and other coordinating groups such as the Programme Management Office. At this level, it should become possible to tackle some of the larger and more time-consuming value-propositions, such as decommissioning large legacy-systems and implementing a full service-oriented architecture.

Enterprise-architecture also begins to be viewed and valued in strategic terms, measured against less-direct business values such as shorter product-development times, increased responsiveness to market changes and shorter time-to-market. Ensure that metrics for realisation and returns on such drivers are included in performance-indicators and success-criteria for the architecture.

Whole-of-enterprise architecture

At this level, there are no further gains from decommissioning, and the real value arises from architecture's role as a cross-functional enabler. The problem is that this value is almost impossible to prove or quantify, because it arises from subtle differences in contexts and connections, and continuous improvements across all aspects of the entire enterprise. As with strategy – in fact *as* strategy – much of the value must be taken on trust.

The danger is that trust alone provides no protection against the dreaded 'bean-counters' and others who are unable to grasp the subtleties of complex systems – those whose understanding is, as one colleague put it, "like that of a child with a drum – cut it open to see what makes the noise". So it's still essential to document whatever demonstrable value does arise, such as from continuing the coordination and 'policing' work of the previous levels.

Procedure

Purpose

Establish frameworks and metrics to monitor impact of enterprise-architecture on whole-of-organisation integration.

People

Enterprise architects, strategists, process architects, IT architects, programme management office, performance specialists.

Preparation

Standard business-analysis tools: whiteboard, meeting-space, pen and paper, time, and access to the required people.

Research on internet and elsewhere for metrics on architecture value-realisation and impact-value monitoring, and methods to elicit them.

Before you start, assess the architecture scope – see *DN :: Architecture of the enterprise* (p.13) – and maturity-level – see *MA :: Measuring maturity* (p.123).

Process

In conjunction with the full team listed above, review the available methods to derive metrics of architecture value to the enterprise, matching the architecture scope and maturity-level.

Select one or more suitable methods. Where appropriate, adapt the metrics to suit the specific needs of the enterprise.

Specify requirements to incorporate the selected metrics into regular reporting, such as a Balanced Scorecard - see *MR :: Real-time scoreboards* (p.112). Pass these requirements to the Programme Management Office, or equivalent, for implementation.

Performance (artefacts and outcomes)

List of required metrics, identifying required data-sources, data-capture processes and business-rules for data-transform.

Broader applications

This perspective is *Performance / Integrated* – a recursive emphasis on overall performance and integration of the whole enterprise.

To paraphrase the questions from the start of this section, how can you demonstrate the overall value of any part of the enterprise? What is each part worth to the enterprise as a whole? Those are the metrics and monitoring-mechanisms we need here.

Resources

📖 David Robertson et al., *Enterprise Architecture as Strategy: creating a foundation for business execution*, Harvard Business School Press, 2006, ISBN-13 978-1591398394

GLOSSARY

This summarises some of the terms and acronyms we've come across in the book.

active learning	systematic process of reflection on action, for the purpose of developing skills and competencies; examples include action-learning/action-research, Quality Circles, debriefing and task self-assessment; link-theme between *mental dimension* and *physical dimension*
ADM	acronym for Architectural Design Method, a methodology used in *TOGAF* to guide development of *enterprise architecture*
appropriate	matching the intended overall purpose; an *EREAI* effectiveness theme associated with the *aspirational dimension* of the context
ArchiMate	a visual language used to model *enterprise architectures*, developed by the Netherlands consortium Telematics
ARIS	acronym for Architecture of Integrated Systems, a production-oriented *enterprise architecture* framework developed by German group IDS-Scheer
aspirational dimension	aspirational and intentional aspects of work and the workplace, expressed in collective and individual identity and *purpose*, and in issues such as ethics, values and codes of conduct; also commitment-assets and aspirational capital such as organisational morale, health and fitness; see also *vision, value; sense-making, foresight, responsibility*
behavioural dimension	see *physical dimension*
chaos domain	in the *Cynefin* model, domain of inherent uncertainty and unpredictability; decisions are guided by *principles* and *values*; represented in the business context by unique market-of-one customisation and by non-repeatable maintenance issues; also useful when deliberately invoked in creativity, in *narrative* and *dialogue,* and in *foresight* techniques such as *scenario* construction

complex domain	in the *Cynefin* model, domain of *emergent* properties and non-linear relationships between factors; decisions are derived from heuristics and guidelines; unlike *chaos*, which is inherently uncertain, may often create an illusion of predictability, especially where linear analysis is applied within a short-term, narrow set of assumptions
conceptual dimension	see *mental dimension*
Cynefin	model of organisational *complexity* developed by David Snowden of Cognitive Edge, which describes four distinct *paradigms* to interpret a given context: *known, knowable, complex* and *chaotic*
dialogue	process of *emergent* conversation in which awareness and knowledge are created between the people the involved; link-theme between *mental dimension* and *emotional dimension*
DyA	Acronym for Dynamic Architecture, an *enterprise-architecture* framework developed by Netherlands consultancy Sogeti
effective	'on purpose', producing the intended result with *optimised* balance over the whole; requires broad generalist awareness of the whole, rather than the narrow focus required to create local efficiency, hence often contrasted with *efficient*
efficient	'doing more with less', creating the maximum result with minimum use or wastage of resources in a specific context; improved incrementally through *active learning* and related techniques for feedback and reflection; major improvements usually require a change in *paradigm*; an *EREAI* theme associated with the *mental dimension* of the context
elegant	human dimensions of *effectiveness*, such as feelings, emotions and ergonomics, expressed in practice in issues such as usability, simplicity and personal preference; an *EREAI* theme associated with the *emotional dimension* of the context
emergence	context within which cause-effect patterns can be identified only retrospectively, and in which analytic techniques are usually unreliable and misleading
emotional dimension	relational and emotional aspects of work and the workspace: feelings and *values*, internal relationships and interpersonal transactions, relationships with external stakeholders; also emotional assets and relational capital such as reputation and trust; see also *vision, value; leadership; narrative, dialogue*
enterprise architecture	a systematic process to model and guide *integration* and *optimisation* of the entire enterprise

EREAI	acronym for five keywords to evaluate effectiveness: *efficient, reliable, elegant, appropriate, integrated*
FEAF	acronym for Federal Enterprise Architecture Framework, a framework and methodology developed for *enterprise architecture* by the US government
foresight	the discipline of developing a forward view in time; link-theme between *aspirational dimension* and *mental dimension*; see also *sense-making; strategy, scenario*
goal	a specific objective to be achieved by a specified point in time; emphasis on the *physical* or *behavioural dimension* of *purpose*, contrasted with *mission, role* and *vision*
integration	contextual awareness of all the interactions between the *physical, mental, emotional* and *aspirational* dimensions of work and the workspace, and the active process of linking them together into a unified whole; an *EREAI* effectiveness theme
knowable domain	in the *Cynefin* model, domain of 'the complicated', with identifiable cause-effect relationships; decisions are derived from contextual analysis
known domain	in the *Cynefin* model, domain of certainty and known cause-effect relationships; decisions are predefined by laws, rules and regulations
leadership	mentoring, coaching, example and other processes for guidance of Self and Other in action; link-theme between *physical dimension* and *emotional dimension*
mental dimension	mental and conceptual aspects of work and the workspace: beliefs, attitudes, knowledge, procedures and process specifications; also knowledge-assets and intellectual capital
mental model	chosen set of beliefs and method to interpret a given context; usually supported by a less-conscious *paradigm* or worldview
mission	a desired capability or state to be achieved, usually within a specified timeframe, and to be maintained indefinitely once achieved; emphasis on the *emotional* and, to a lesser extent, the *mental dimensions* of *purpose*, contrasted with *goal, role* and *vision*
narrative	personalised and often emotive expression or interpretation of knowledge, as history, anecdote or story; link-theme between *mental dimension* and *emotional dimension*

optimisation   process of *integration* in which *efficiency* in different areas is traded-off and balanced for maximum *effectiveness* over the whole; in any complex or layered context, the process relies extensively on the *EREAI* themes (*efficient, reliable, elegant, appropriate, integrated*) to identify the energies and resources to be balanced, and on the R^5 principles (*recursion, rotation, reflexion, reciprocation, resonance*) to identify balances and trade-offs between different layers and sub-contexts such as departments, business processes and business units

paradigm   coherent set of beliefs about cause-effect relationships within a given class of context

physical dimension   physical aspects of work and the workspace: skills, competencies, physical processes, behaviours, actions; also tangible assets and work-environment

power   the ability to do *work* or, in some contexts, the rate at which work is done; in a collective sense, the ability to get work done; in human terms, this definition needs to be expanded as the ability to work, play, relate, learn, as an expression of personal choice, personal responsibility and personal purpose and with awareness and respect of shared purpose

practical dimension   see *physical dimension*

principle   a conceptual commitment or model, the *mental-dimension* equivalent of *value*

purpose   an expression of individual and/or collective identity - the *aspirational* theme of "who we are and what we stand for"; incorporates distinct dimensions of *vision, role, mission* and *goal*

R^5 collective term for five characteristics of *complex*-systems used in the *tetradian* model of *integration*, namely *recursion, rotation, reflexion, reciprocation* and *resonance*

reciprocation   overall balance in transactions, especially *power*-transactions; reciprocal balance between entities is not necessarily direct or immediate, and in many cases balance may only be achieved over time at a system-wide level, with energy-transfers occurring between *physical, mental, emotional* and/or *aspirational* dimensions; an R^5 principle for assessment of *effectiveness* and relevance

recursion	patterns of relationship or interaction repeat or are 'self-similar' at different scales; permits simplification of otherwise complex processes; an R^5 principle for assessment of *effectiveness* and relevance
reflexion	corollary of *recursion*, in that the whole, or aspects of the whole, can be identified within the attributes and transactions of any part at any scale; an R^5 principle for assessment of *effectiveness* and relevance
relational dimension	see *emotional dimension*
reliable	high degree of certainty and predictability for a desired outcome; an *EREAI* theme associated with the *physical dimension* of a context
resonance	the 'snowball effect' in all real-world systems, balancing feedback and feedforward (increasing the effect towards *self-propagation*) against damping (reducing the effect); an R^5 principle for assessment of *effectiveness* and relevance
responsibility	literally 'response-ability', the ability to choose and act upon appropriate responses according to context, as an expression of personal *power*; link-theme between *aspirational dimension* and *physical dimension*
role	a declared focus or *strategic* position within the 'world' described by a *vision*; emphasis on the *conceptual* or *mental* and, to a lesser extent, the *emotional* dimensions of *purpose*, contrasted with *goal, mission* and *vision*
rotation	systematic process of assessing a context from multiple perspectives; an R^5 principle for assessment of *effectiveness* and relevance
scenario	an imagined future context, developed for the purpose of understanding both the present context and options for action in the future context; a *foresight* technique
self-propagation	aspect of *integration* in which a meme – an idea, a practice, a way of relating or the like – spreads throughout an organisation, requiring little or no effort or intervention beyond the initial 'seeding'; contrasted with the more typical 'command-and-control' *tactics*, which require constant effort and intervention to impose a meme throughout the organisation; may be either constructive or destructive
SEMPER	acronym for *Spiritual, Emotional, Mental, Physical, Effectiveness* (*EREAI*), Relevance (R^5); also the Latin word for 'always'

sense-making the process of creating *mental models* to provide a conceptual framework for understanding ambiguity, *emergence* and uncertainty; link-theme between *aspirational dimension* and *mental dimension*; see also *foresight*

'start anywhere' principle corollary of *self-propagation*, in that 'seeding' for *integration* may be started from any appropriate aspect of the organisation, permitting different types of pilot projects to be trialled simultaneously in multiple areas – usually away from nominal 'problems' – allowing *emergence* to indicate 'winners' for further *self-propagation*

strategy 'big picture' view of an action-plan to implement a *purpose*, usually emphasising the *vision, role* and *mission* components; contrasted with the *tactics* required to execute the plan

tactics detailed *missions, goals* and other step-by-step activities to execute a *strategy*, or some segment of an overall strategy

tetradian (alt. tetradion) depiction of the *physical, mental, emotional* and *aspirational* dimensions as four axes in a tetrahedral relationship, usually also showing the respective link-themes as the edges between the vertices of the tetrahedron

TOGAF acronym for The Open Group Architecture Framework, a framework and methodology for IT-oriented *enterprise architecture* developed by the Open Group consortium

value an emotional commitment; link-theme between *aspirational dimension* and *emotional dimension*

vision description of a desired 'world', always far greater than any individual or organization; described in the present tense, yet never 'achieved'; emphasis on the *aspirational dimension* of *purpose*, contrasted with *goal, mission* and *role*; also link-theme between *aspirational dimension* and *emotional dimension*

visioning generic term for process to identify, develop and document *vision* and *values*, leading towards *strategy* and *tactics*

work the activity of changing energy from one form to another; in human terms, the exchange may be between any forms of *physical, mental, emotional* and/or *aspirational* energy

Zachman framework a systematic structure for categorisation of models within an IT-oriented *enterprise architecture*, developed by John Zachman